Letters to Juliet

Julietta of Verona

Verona

Italia

Lise Friedman & Ceil Friedman

Stewart, Tabori & Chang
New York

To Tony and Erminio, con amore

Published in 2006 by Stewart, Tabori & Chang
An imprint of ABRAMS

Library of Congress Cataloging-in-Publication Data
Friedman, Lise.
 Letters to Juliet : celebrating Shakespeare's greatest heroine, the magical city of
Verona, and the power of love / by Lise Friedman and Ceil Friedman.
  p. cm.
 ISBN 13: 978-1-58479-912-2
 1. Juliet (Fictitious character). 2. Shakespeare, William, 1564–1616. Romeo and
Juliet. 3. Club di Giulietta (Verona, Italy). I. Friedman, Ceil. II. Title.
PR2831.F75 2006
822.3'3—dc22

EDITOR: Jennifer Eiss
DESIGNER: Laura Lindgren
PRODUCTION MANAGER: Jacquie Poirier

The text of this book was composed in Pastonchi

Printed and bound in U.S.A.
10 9 8 7 6 5 4 3 2 1

Stewart, Tabori & Chang books are available at special discounts when
purchased in quantity for premiums and promotions as well as fundraising or
educational use. Special editions can also be created to specification. For
details, contact specialsales@abramsbooks.com or the address below.

THE ART OF BOOKS SINCE 1949
115 West 18th Street
New York, NY 10011
www.abramsbooks.com

Contents

西省水利…

朱丽叶小姐

好!

…是一个中学生，今年已经16岁了，在这个充满
…的理想，有自己的爱好，但是也时常感
…如所措。

我爱好文学，集邮都是我的业余爱好。因此
…好的朋友。我爱幻想，也爱冒险，有…
…有图书馆里发现了《罗米欧与朱丽叶》，…
…爱情的悲剧深深地被他们的追求深深的…
…们自觉地拼命运而感到惊讶，也对他…
…而感到愤慨。我热爱生活，也…
…不明白，为什么生活中好人一生不平安呢？…
…幸福罗米欧与朱丽叶时代价们能够在天…

…中国和意大利人民自古以来就热爱…
…友聪明。我爱我们的祖国，深深地热…
…我很想把我们的祖国介绍给你…
…洋西季，流千黄河流域，蜿蜒和黄海…
…地的象征长安，国代表牡丹，风鸟瑞秀…
…桂林山水，有奇峻险拔的五岳，以及栩栩如生的战城…
…还有与罕义大型的秦始皇兵马俑，济南的趵突泉，西安的华…
…也都很有名，我代表我们的国际和您，邀请您…

第　頁

لم عليكم. انا اسمي بيان نارپيان جمال

…تلك عاطفية والحقيقة هي مشكلة تدوري اكثر من عائلة
…من خمسة سنوات اهب فتاة واعتقد ولكن لاذنتم
…اكثر من مره صارحتباحبي واكبرا كانت تستجزء
…وتقول لي انك صديق شهرآ و نقصد صديق الجميع
…بدافتي ان اعترمن فتلي لدخول على هيرا وانا منذ
…ممارستي رياضة بناء الدجام وهوم الرياضة قاسيه جدآ
…ملتها وكني مقممارسو هزه الرياضة يجب استقال
…تاميتات خاصة ببناء الاهبام وتزم الفيتامينات
…فود عودنا بسبب الحصار على بلدي العراق
…ارجوا منكم ان نرسلوا لي هزه الفيتامينات
…ممارسة رياضة بناء الاهبام وشكرآ
…التي اعتقها وشكرآ

993/01
14/15 ans

Chère Juliette,

Nous sommes 2 françaises de 14 et 15 ans,
Coline et Marion. Nous t'écrivons car nous pensons
que t'as vécu la plus belle histoire d'amour de
tous les temps et que tu as fait preuve d'un courage
exceptionnel. En effet, te tuer pour Roméo! Nous sommes
sûres que vous vous êtes retrouvés au paradis de
l'amour vous êtes réunis pour l'éternité, sans
parents. Juliette, serait-il possible
…envoie une photo de ton tombeau
…an à Vérone? Nous te remercions
…Peux-tu nous rendre un dernier service
…les cieux, William Shakespeare pour
…merveilleuse histoire.

Nadine

…art Marion
…des papillons

BRUSSELS 27/9

♥ 2024/00

DEAR JULIET,

I am really in love (and it is
the first time) with a spanish boy
living in MADRID. He is 34, he
has wonderful brown eyes and he
is romantic. My question is, Juliet
do you think I should quit and
leave all my family - job - flat - cat
and friends... here in Belgium to
go to his village to live with
him? as I can not stay here anymore.
I love him so much! What do you
think? Please, help me. "Grazie mile"
(I'm also a teacher 34)

His name is LUCIEN   ♥   KATRINA T°
He is romantic, nice,   84 HELLDAL
cute, funny, clever   1863 BRUSSELS
I love him   Belgium

♥ write soon Juliet
please…

Venezia 8 gennaio 1998

G. came

70

ercevolmente colpita…
…sono piacevolmente

…sino
…giornato di gennaio. mi ha
…o nel mio cuc…
…espresso la mi…rio
…nel mio intin…a, eno
…bre…ella notte
…lena di m…
…a… e su una…
…chica, che ti v…
…no belli…

My Sweetest Juliet,

How fairest thou, my love?
…do so wish with all of myself
…at thou art well, for if my beauteous
…liet were not, despair would settle
…avily upon my heart. Oh, Juliet, the
…s do pass so tediously without your
…your love. My eyes long to behold
…lovely presence. It seems twelve
…rs since we did last meet, though
…ly a meat day. I knowest that thou
…he same, for we are one in thought.
…merry, my sweet, and do not allow
…thoughts to lessen your beauty with
…wn, for the day draws nigh when we
…again meet. On the dawn of Thursday
…ve be united, forevermore to be
…er in our happiness, away from
…y of our kinsmen.

…en though mine eyes are forced to
…ok upon your face for the while, I
…ave the beautiful image of your face
…ed within my memory. When I gaze
…e stars at night, they remind me of
…two bright stars that say my
…your eyes which…

Introduction

Dear Juliet,
I know that you will take a long time to answer me, but
that's not important—I adore talking to a legend. When
I received your first letter, I felt uplifted by a divine force,
ready to help me and sustain me. Today, I need you to
listen to me once again.

✦

*L*ike most siblings, we are always on the lookout for an excuse to finish each other's sentences, a habit we've been perfecting since early childhood. Our routine took on new meaning some years ago, when one of us (Ceil) left New York to be with her own Romeo in, of all places, Verona. Like almost everyone we knew, we had abandoned the art of letter writing for the immediacies of email, dashing off almost daily messages to each other about whatever happened to cross our minds: children, husbands, parents, what to make for dinner, and, as time went on, our desire to work together. So when we came across the lines above, written by a nineteen-year-old French woman, as well as excerpts from several other letters to Juliet, we couldn't resist digging further.

Who were these people who took the time to write, and why did they care so much about a character in a play? Our investigation led us first to the Club di Giulietta, a volunteer organization in Verona whose multiple "secretaries" reply to the thousands of letters that arrive each year addressed to the Shakespearean heroine. We learned that the tradition of writing to Juliet dates to the early twentieth century, and that someone—at times more than one person—has replied to these letters since the 1930s.

We then explored libraries in Verona and New York City, poring over the first historical and literary references to the Romeo and Juliet story. We followed the trail through the nineteenth and early twentieth centuries, when writers from Verona and abroad, Charles Dickens and Lord Byron among them, recorded their impressions of the sites linked to the legend.

Our timing couldn't have been better. The son and daughter, respectively, of Juliet's first and second "official" secretaries are alive and well living in Verona and, from the moment we approached them, were eager to supply us with oral histories, articles, photographs, and ephemera crucial to the patching together of the early history of the letter writing phenomenon.

Subsequent "Juliets" were equally obliging, sharing insights that reflect the period during which they were active, and telling us how they initially became involved. Some had particular language skills. Some were pinch hitters, recruited by a desperate city over-

 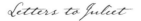

whelmed with unanswered letters. Still others pursued the role, drawn to the task out of passion for the story and empathy with the correspondents.

The result is that for seven decades and counting, an almost unbroken chain of secretaries has lovingly attended Juliet's letters. Their commitment to keeping her legend alive has inspired each of them to spend a few minutes (or hours) each day responding to the requests for advice, pleas for compassion and understanding, and desires for a blessing from Shakespeare's most romantic leading lady. Juliet is no longer just a heroine in a story but has gone beyond literary constraints to assume the roles of adviser and confidante.

The letters range from the baroque, teeming with breathless and extravagant prose, to the intimate and chatty, to the matter-of-fact, free of excess or flourishes. With few exceptions, they come across as sincere. They are from adolescents struggling with parental censure and the unforgiving throes of a first love, and from adults— young and old—celebrating a hard-won love, wrestling with commitment, betrayal, and loss, and confronting the vagaries of religion, politics, and race.

They arrive by the truckload, from all over the world, in almost every imaginable language—composed on ornate stationery, scrawled on loose-leaf, or scribbled quickly on scraps of whatever paper was handy when the urge struck. The secretaries read, often translate, and answer each one, personally and by hand. Frequently addressed simply, "Juliet, Verona," all of these letters reach their destination.

Shakespeare, after all, did not choose Verona casually. The legend has merged with the city's history since 1524, when the Italian author Luigi da Porto first set the tale in fourteenth-century Verona and named the protagonists Romeo and Giulietta. Juliet's tomb has attracted innumerable pilgrimages of believers as well as plenty of skeptics. And the crowds that flock to her house are second in size only to those that visit the city's number one tourist attraction, the unequivocally authentic Roman arena. Shakespeare's retelling of the story ensured its worldwide fame, but Juliet belongs to Verona.

Whether her character was a fanciful composite of all the runaway emotions that accompany a forbidden first love or based on a real person is a source of endless speculation. (Perhaps there is something to the saying that legends come about when the truth is considered too dangerous.) What is not in dispute is the powerful hold Juliet has on everyone who encounters her.

Once we had Juliet in mind, evidence of her influence began to turn up in the unlikeliest of places. Verona's annual numismatic fair was maybe the most improbable of all. It was one of those freezing November mornings that demands an indoor activity engrossing enough to occupy two young boys and not drive their parents and visiting aunt crazy. After much casting about—nothing good playing at the movies, a resounding "no" to yet another trip to the museums—a quick glance through the local paper provided the solution. The coin exposition! Perfect. It took place at the nearby trade fair center and offered, at minimum, a good two hours of indoor entertainment.

Predictably, the fair was packed. While the boys and their father moved happily from booth to booth, we went off to see what else, if anything, might be on display. A few minutes of wandering led us to an area set aside for vendors selling old prints and postcards. There were thousands of items to look through, organized by theme and geographical location.

We zeroed in on a pile of old postcards highlighting sites in and around Verona—Piazza delle Erbe filled with vegetable stands, the Arena, Castelvecchio, the Romanesque facade of the Duomo. There were also many postcards related to the legend of Romeo and Juliet. Mixed in with wonderfully torrid Pre-Raphaelite paintings of the emblematic balcony and death scenes were a handful of early-twentieth-century photos and engravings of Juliet's house and court-yard and a few heavily atmospheric shots of her tomb site.

One in particular caught our attention. A young woman wearing a long dark skirt, her hair covered by a black scarf, kneels in prayer at one end of what is clearly Juliet's tomb. Someone shot it not in this past century, but in the late 1890s; we had stumbled across the earli-est known photograph of the site. The woman's reverence is compel-ling enough, but it's what surrounds her that startled us. Fastened to the brick wall behind the sarcophagus, its base littered with broken bits of columns, are hundreds of notes and mementos—confirma-tion that the urge to communicate with Juliet is nothing new.

2683 **Verona – *Tomba***
Giulietta e Romeo

JULIET'S TOMB, LATE NINETEENTH CENTURY

Dear Juliet,
Who knows who will read these messages, who will be
curious to know the desires of strangers? Story or legend,
it isn't rhetoric…because Juliet exists. Yes, you exist and
this is a prayer that every day, more and more, you will be
in me and in the heart of every man, and that you make
him a dreamer, or lover, that you make him come alive!

ITALY

I've asked myself many times, how it is that we fall in love: do we trip, lose our balance and fall, scraping our hearts? Do we crash to the ground, on stones? Or it is like staying on the edge of a precipice for all time?

POLAND

❧

My name is Riccardo. I am ten years old and live in a town in a province of Mantua. Last summer I met a pretty fourteen-year-old girl who lives in Verona, named Federica. I would like very much to see her again. Can you give me any news of her?

ITALY

❧

Dear Juliet,
You are my last hope. The woman I love more than anything in the world has left me. You, who are the purest of women, and who understands what real love is, I beg you, do something for me: write to her and tell her that I love her, that I will always love her, that she is my life. I know that it is possible for you to do anything, since you know what it means to die for love.

FRANCE

ONE OF THE MANY NOTES LEFT
AT JULIET'S TOMB

CHAPTER ONE

The Story Behind the Story

Two households, both alike in dignity,
(In fair Verona, where we lay our scene)
From ancient grudge break to new mutiny,
Where civil blood makes civil hands unclean.
From forth the fatal loins of these two foes
A pair of star-cross'd lovers take their life,
Whose misadventur'd piteous overthrows
Doth with their death bury their parents' strife.

—PROLOGUE, *Romeo and Juliet*

Shakespeare's searing drama may be the world's most widely known story of tragic love, but it certainly wasn't the first. Orpheus and Eurydice. Tristan and Isolde. Lancelot and Guinevere.

L'addio di Romeo a Giulietta (OIL ON CANVAS), FRANCESCO HAYEZ, 1823

There is no shortage of tales of young love thwarted by fatal miscues or plain bad luck. Granted, Shakespeare took things a bit further with *Romeo and Juliet*, including in his story a death-simulating potion and a chilling double suicide. But like all enduring legends, his too has deep roots.

Scholars trace elements of *Romeo and Juliet* as far back as ancient Rome, to Ovid's *Pyramus and Thisbe*, a bittersweet tale of feuding families, forbidden love, and a secret meeting at a tomb gone terribly wrong. While waiting for Pyramus, Thisbe catches sight of a roving lioness. Fearing that the animal's bloody jaws are evidence of her lover's slaying, Thisbe flees to a nearby cave, her scarf falling to the ground. The lioness then discovers the scarf and, smelling human flesh, slashes it to pieces.

Meanwhile, a frantic Pyramus finds the shredded and bloody remnant. Certain his lover has been killed, he stabs himself. Just moments later, Thisbe emerges from her hiding place and discovers Pyramus on the brink of death, her scarf in his hands. One glance at her and he is gone.

Mad with grief, Thisbe grabs Pyramus's sword. She utters the words, "Thy own hand has slain thee, and for my sake I too can be brave for once . . . I will follow thee in death, for I have been the cause; and death which alone could part us shall not prevent my joining thee," and kills herself while bending over Pyramus's still-warm body. Their sensational deaths, like those of Shakespeare's Romeo and Juliet, lead to the reconciliation of the two families. (Tellingly, perhaps, the lovers make a comedic cameo appearance in *A Midsummer Night's Dream*.)

Pyramus and Thisbe (OIL ON CANVAS), GREGORIO PAGANI, 1600

Writing a century or two after Ovid, Xenophon of Ephesus further anticipates Shakespeare with the melodramatic *An Ephesian Tale*. Beautiful Anthia and the equally dazzling Habrocomes are literally sickened by their unconsummated love. Their mystified parents seek the help of Apollo, whose oracle dictates they marry and be sent abroad.

Naturally, it's no ordinary journey; in fact, it verges on the preposterous. Pirates, imprisonment, beatings, and attempted murder all figure in the countless (and unsuccessful) assaults on the newlyweds' virtue. At one particularly fraught juncture Anthia, desperate to avoid a forced marriage, takes what she believes to be poison but is in fact a sleeping potion. She eventually wakes up in a tomb. Not to be outdone by his bride's misadventures, Habrocomes survives, among other indignities, a shipwreck and a crucifixion. As it turns out, their love and, miraculously, their lives prevail.

Even more direct antecedents to Shakespeare's play turn up in a number of fifteenth- and sixteenth-century Italian stories. Masuccio Salernitano surely knew of Xenophon's tale before writing the thirty-third story of his popular 1476 *Cinquante Novelle*, in which a bribed friar secretly weds the hapless Sienese lovers Mariotto and Giannozza. Shortly after their marriage, Mariotto accidentally kills an important citizen during a brawl and is banished to Alexandria. Overwhelmed by the loss of her new husband, Giannozza concocts a risky plan to meet him. She tells her father that she will marry one of her numerous suitors, then immediately sends for the friar.

Initially reluctant to get involved, he's persuaded by her weeping and agrees to give her a potion that "would not only make her sleep

Letters to Juliet

for three days, but seem to be really dead." Buried by her duped and grieving family, then rescued by the friar, she escapes to Alexandria . . . but not before pirates capture the messenger she had dispatched to tell Mariotto of her scheme. Believing Giannozza is dead he rushes to Siena and attempts to pry open her tomb, only to be caught and beheaded. Learning that Mariotto was killed while trying to mourn her passing, a bereft Giannozza returns home to enter a convent and, ultimately, succumbs to heartbreak.

A half century later, soldier-turned-writer Luigi da Porto responded to Masuccio with *Historia novellamente ritrovata di due nobili amanti* (*A Newly Discovered Story of Two Noble Lovers*), published posthumously in 1530. He transported the tale from Siena to Verona, set it during the brief reign (1301–1304) of the Veronese ruler Bartolomeo della Scala, and introduced the names of the rival Montecchi and Cappelletti families. The well-read da Porto claimed he heard his version of the story from one of his bowmen, Pellegrino of Verona, and never directly acknowledged that these names first appeared together in Canto VI of Dante's *Purgatory.*

FRONTISPIECE FOR LUIGI DA PORTO'S *NOVELLA NOVA-MENTE RITROVATA D'UNA INNAMORAMENTO . . . ,* VENICE, 1535

Whatever his source, da Porto established both the story's basic shape and many of the characters that appeared approximately sixty-seven years later in Shakespeare's play. The lovers, Romeo and Giulietta, meet at a masked ball at the house of Cappelletti: "From the moment [Giulietta] gazed on him . . . his beauty so enthralled her entire being that when their eyes first met, her feelings were no longer under her control."

Romeo is no less enamored. Furtive meetings lead to a secret marriage conducted by the benevolent, but somewhat self-serving, Friar Lorenzo, who hopes the lovers' union will bring peace between the rival families (and it wouldn't hurt his standing if the prince recognized his critical role in the happy outcome). The peace the friar craves eventually does come, but at a tremendous cost: Romeo kills Giulietta's cousin Tebaldo in a brawl and is banished.

In the meantime, Giulietta's parents have promised her to the Count of Lodrone. Distraught, she turns to the friar, and, ever obliging, he ministers a potion that induces symptoms of death. A letter detailing Giulietta's plan fails to reach Romeo, and after hearing of her demise he returns to Verona disguised as a peasant. Mistaking his beloved's uncannily deep sleep for death, he reasons that life is not worth living without his true love and poisons himself. Giulietta wakes just in time to see her lover expire and, in a fit of extreme adolescent angst, somehow manages to hold her breath until she also dies. Horrified by the consequences of their animosity, the families reconcile.

Da Porto's action-packed novella was so popular that before long multiple versions followed. A significant interpretation came from

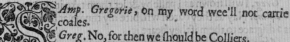

THE MOST EXCEL-
LENT AND LAMENTABLE
Hiſtorie of R O M E O and
J U L I E T.

Enter Sampſon *and* Gregorie *with Swords and Bucklers,*
of the Houſe of Capulet.

Samp. Gregorie, on my word wee'll not carrie
coales.

Greg. No, for then we ſhould be Colliers.

Samp. I meane, and we be in choler wee'll draw.

Greg. I, while you live draw your necke out of the
collar.

Samp. I ſtrike quickly being moved.

Greg. But thou art not quickly moved to ſtrike.

Samp. A dogge of the houſe of *Mountague* moves me.

Greg. To move is to ſtirre, and to be valiant is to ſtand,
Therefore if thou art moved thou runn'ſt away.

Samp. A dogge of that houſe ſhall move me to ſtand.
I will take the wall of any man or maide of *Mountagues*.

Greg. That ſhewes thee a weake ſlave, for the weakeſt goes
to the wall.

Samp. 'Tis true, and therefore women being the weaker veſ-
ſels are ever thruſt to the wall : therefore I will puſh *Mounta-*
gues men from the wall, and thruſt his maides to the wall.

Greg. The quarrell is between our Maſters and us their men.

Samp. 'Tis all one, I will ſhew my ſelfe a Tyrant, when I have
fought with the men I will be cruell with the maids, I will cut off
their heads.

Greg. The heads of the maids!

A 2   Samp.

Romeo and Juliet, ACT I, SCENE I, WILLIAM SHAKESPEARE

Matteo Bandello. A monk who preferred the luxe life at court to the relative austerity of the cloister, Bandello traveled extensively around Italy before finally moving to France, where he assumed the post of Bishop of Aven and wrote many stories. In 1532 he was a guest at the villa of Cesare Fregoso in the town of Caldiero, a fashionable retreat near Verona known for its medicinal waters. Bandello's tale begins with an introduction recalling how visitors from surrounding cities would gather and trade stories in the convivial atmosphere of the baths. Among these raconteurs, he says, was "Captain Alessandro Peregrino, who narrated a pitiful story that took place in Verona at the time of Signor Bartolomeo della Scala." Bandello's rendering yields Book IX of his 1554 *Novelle*.

Bandello echoed da Porto to a large extent, though among other changes he played up the families' antagonism and introduced the complicitous nurse. He also had Romeo refuse Giulietta's wish to flee with him to Mantua, a bad decision that sends Giulietta running to the friar for help. A plague quarantine waylays the messenger bringing news of the potion. A misinformed, and apparently maladroit, Romeo fails to kill himself with a sword and, returning to Verona, makes his way to Giulietta's tomb. There, he downs poison from a vial stashed in his cloak. As he's fading, Giulietta suddenly wakes and the lovers share precious, desperate moments before Romeo dies. Unable to go on, Giulietta literally wills herself to die. Their deaths bring peace between the families, yet unlike the resolution in da Porto's rendition the accord is short-lived.

While da Porto's story achieved great popularity in his native

Italy, it was Frenchman Pierre Boaistuau's morally robust translation of Bandello in 1559 that launched the tale on its journey across the continent to England, where Shakespeare granted it immortality.

But first, two other Englishmen had their turns. In 1567, William Painter described the events in his much-appropriated *Palace of Pleasure*. Five years earlier Arthur Brooke relied heavily on Boaistuau for his *Tragicall Historye of Romeus and Juliet*, a sprawling 3020-line poem considered Shakespeare's primary source.

Though Brooke's narrative for the most part holds fast to Boaistuau's, like his predecessors he felt compelled to put his imprint on the tale. He granted more weight to the star-crossed aspect of the lovers' story, reduced Juliet's age by two years from da Porto's eighteen ("Scarce saw she yet full sixteen years: too young to be a bride!"), gave greater importance and the gift of gab to the nurse, and increased the duration of key incidents. (Shakespeare, in turn, reimagined his Juliet as a pubescent thirteen, further enhanced the nurse's pivotal role, and compressed Brooke's leisurely unfolding of events into a tumultuous four or five days.) According to many scholars, Brooke also made liberal use of Chaucer's seminal *Troilus and Criseyde*, a work that Shakespeare further mined.

Debate still rages regarding Shakespeare's firsthand knowledge of the Italian novellas. Scholars tend to agree that da Porto supplied the core themes and Brooke the scaffold. All the controversy surrounding the legend's evolution aside, what's incontestable is that, through the eloquence and urgency of his language, Shakespeare transformed a colorful story into the tour de force we know as *Romeo and Juliet*.

Dear Juliet,

My name is of no importance, for what's in a name? However, I do have a problem that I'm hoping you can solve. I'm a fifteen-year-old male whose life is almost like Romeo and Juliet's would have been if they lived in our time. I have the feelings of love at first sight, being lied to and cheated on (Rosaline and Romeo), and the urge to love another with my full attention and heart. Are these feelings a problem? And if they are, what should I do?

Sincerely,
(unknown)

Dear Juliet,

I really didn't understand your character. You were so impetuous at your young age. How could you fall in love after one kiss and two minutes? And why did you kill yourself instead of living on with the memory of Romeo? When Romeo was banished, why didn't you try to hide him? If you had, he would be alive now, and so would you.

Do you regret the decision you made?

I am looking forward to your answer. Thanks.

Sincerely,
Warren M., DULUTH, MINNESOTA

Dear Juliet,

Once again a San Valentino without Valentino. I am
no longer waiting for my knight in shining armor,
and I am thoroughly discouraged. Most of my friends
think I'm nuts because I still believe in fairy tales and
romantic stories. Some time ago I began to think, and
still do, that because I'm not very pretty no man would
ever look at me with admiration. Since I work a lot and
have strict parents, I rarely go out. I am twenty-five and
I often dream that one day, while serving a client, a
stranger will walk through the door and take me away,
and I will turn into a beautiful butterfly. I am looking
for a job in another field so I can become independent
and not depend on my parents. If you can help me, I will
be very grateful.

Affectionately,
Miriam F., Glasgow, Scotland

CHAPTER TWO

The Tomb Site

Come, come with me and we will make short work,
For, by your leaves, you shall not stay alone
Till holy church incorporate two in one.

FRIAR LAURENCE, ACT II, SCENE VI

*I*n 1230, in a bucolic setting not far from Verona's Adige River, the Frati Minori Francescani founded a church dedi-cated to their recently deceased patron saint, who had paused here about ten years earlier. It was within a small chapel of this church, known as San Francesco al Corso, that Friar Laurence performed the rushed, clandestine marriage of Romeo and Juliet and, a scant four days later, mourned their deaths in the nearby Capulet family crypt.

But first, back to the facts. Just four decades after its founding, the Franciscans abandoned their modest sanctuary, which had grown to include a convent and gardens, for the more prestigious Church

JULIET'S TOMB, VIEW OF CLOISTER, 1940S

of San Fermo. The complex then passed to the Order of San Marco of Mantua, a sect that included both monks and nuns. (Shakespeare and a few of his literary predecessors indulged in a bit of artistic license, placing the Franciscan friar here in the historically impossible year 1303. An actual friar would have followed his order to its new seat.)

The order's ranks thinned over the years, and by 1336 the few remaining nuns had taken Benedictine vows. In the mid-sixteenth century the convent was turned over to an order commonly known as the Franceschine, its occupants when the first historical reference to the tomb appears:

> The bodies of the unfortunate lovers were, by their common will, placed in the same monument, which of vivid stone was considerably above ground, and which I have seen used over and over as a basin at the well of those poor wards of S. Francesco, while the site was being renovated for them; and pondering this fact with Cava-lier Gerardo Boldiero, my uncle, who introduced me to that place, showing me not only the aforementioned sepulcher, but also a site in the wall . . . where, as he affirms to have understood, this tomb, with some ashes and bones, was removed many years ago.

Girolamo dalla Corte's description, from Book X of his *Istoria della Città di Verona*, seems oddly matter-of-fact, considering the disposal of the tomb's apparently heretical contents. (The uncle dalla Corte refs to was, incidentally, the pseudonymous "Clizia, nobile Veronese," author of a popular variation on the Romeo and Juliet theme composed in poetic verse and published in 1553.)

Almost nothing more was written about the tomb for the next two centuries. It somehow survived the massive explosion of a nearby munitions deposit in 1624 that destroyed the church, which was rebuilt one year later. Despite the long silence, dalla Corte's chronicle had a lasting impact. Looking back, in his 1889 *Cenni Storici sulla Tomba di Giulietta e Romeo in Verona* (Historical References to the Tomb of Juliet and Romeo in Verona), the historian Antonio Zambelli wonders if Luigi da Porto's *A Newly Discovered Story of Two Noble Lovers* may have brought too much notoriety to the catastrophic tale of the lovers' suicides.

"It is well known," he writes, "that suicides, equated with those guilty of homicide, were refused church burial; they were instead buried like animals. When in 1303 the event occurred, out of regard for their families, who were rich and powerful in Verona, the Ecclesiastical Authorities tolerated their burial at a sacred site, but in a tomb without coats of arms or inscriptions.

"What is certain, because it is narrated by the contemporary historian dalla Corte, is that around 1548 the tomb was profaned and placed on the floor to collect water. For this purpose those crude holes, still visible, were made to let the water flow out. Its cover was destroyed." If so, then how to explain the remark by the nineteenth-century playwright August von Kotzebue that he had seen the cover while visiting Johannes, archduke of Austria?

By the early 1800s the site attracted an increasing number of pilgrims eager to venerate the tomb, now identified solely with the Shakespearean heroine. (Curiously, as the adoration of Juliet increased over time, Romeo's "presence" was no longer required.) Their reverence often involved swiping bits of the crumbling sarcophagus—as keepsakes or to fashion into jewelry. Yet no one stepped in to protect the object of their devotion.

Tourists weren't the only visitors to help themselves to souvenirs. When the stylish Marie-Louise of Austria, duchess of Parma and Napoleon's second wife, visited the site in the 1820s she reportedly commissioned a necklace and earrings made of fragments chiseled from the tomb and set in gold. It wasn't long before enterprising merchants got into the act. One historian describes a savvy jeweler in Verona's Piazza delle Erbe who did a brisk business in red marble nuggets that he had pried from columns near his shop. Clearly amused by the man's ingenuity, he reasons that "this was certainly not fraud, since both the columns and the venerated tomb were made of the same marble."

Not all visitors intended to raid the tomb. Many were simply eager to satisfy their curiosity. A visit in 1816 by Lord Byron produced the following observation:

> Of the truth of Juliet's story they [the Veronese] seem tenacious to a degree, insisting on the fact—giving a date (1303), and showing a tomb. It is a plain, open, and partly decayed sarcophagus, with withered leaves in it, in a wild and desolate conventual garden, once a cemetery, now

ruined to the very graves. The situation struck me as very appropriate to the legend, being blighted as their love.

His lofty prose aside, temptation got the best of Byron as well. He admits that he "brought away a few pieces of the granite, to give to my daughter and my nieces."

An equally smitten Charles Dickens describes his Veronese experience, one stop on the Grand Tour, in his 1846 *Pictures from Italy*.

Charles Dickens (DRYPOINT), Alfred Guillaume Gabriel Orsay, 1845

> So, I went off, with a guide, to an old, old garden, once belonging to an old, old convent, I suppose; and being admitted, at a shattered gate, by a bright-eyed woman who was washing clothes, went down some walks where fresh plants and young flowers were prettily growing among fragments of old wall, and ivy-coloured mounds; and was shown a little tank, or water trough, which the bright-eyed woman drying her arms upon her 'kerchief, called "La tomba di Giulietta la sfortunata." With the best disposition in the world to believe, I could do no more than believe that the bright-eyed woman believed; so I gave her that much credit, and her customary fee in ready money.

These nineteenth-century impressions underscore the tomb's lure despite the site's physical degradation, which only worsened when the cloister became state property following the Napoleonic decrees and during the successive Austrian occupation.

By the time the Congregazione di Carità (Congregation of Charity) took over the complex in 1868, popular belief in the tomb's veracity showed no signs of letting up. The new tenants must have realized this. They placed the tomb against a wall beneath a portico, in a site patched together with remnants of the ancient church walls and other elements from the original monastery. They also installed stone plaques commemorating the seventeenth-century explosion and rebuilding of the church, along with a number of antique tomb-stones. This enclosure, surrounded by an iron gate, attracted visitors who came to honor Juliet and to leave greetings and ex-votos tacked to the wall behind the tomb.

In 1898 the Verona city council voted to create more "decorous surroundings"; photographs taken early in the twentieth century show that this consisted of a Romanesque arcade built around the marble relic, now moved away from the wall and elevated on a stone base. Little else changed for nearly four decades other than the placement, with much fanfare, in 1910 of a marble bust of Shakespeare by the Veronese artist Renato Cattani in the nearby garden. While still a magnet for tourists, the site was undeniably squalid.

Things declined as the century progressed. Visitors to the tomb and the deconsecrated convent of San Francesco al Corso had to trudge through the adjoining agricultural fairgrounds, where horse

JULIET'S TOMB, EARLY 1900S

traders and cattle breeders carried out their business. And so it went until 1937, when Antonio Avena, director of the Verona Civic Museums, took on the task of giving it an appearance more deserving of the story. He was without question inspired by the success of George Cukor's 1936 film *Romeo and Juliet*, a consummate Hollywood extravaganza that had recently premiered in Verona (dubbed in Italian).

Anticipating the huge potential for Verona's tourism business, Avena decided to recast the principal monuments in a romantic mold that would meet visitors' expectations. Actually, not a single frame of the Cukor movie was filmed in Verona, or anywhere else in Italy. The director had instead sent an advance team of experts to Italy to scout locales, which they recorded in reams of drawings,

PRE-WORLD WAR II WALKWAY LEADING TO JULIET'S TOMB

annotated sketches, and photographs. Cukor used these to create his sets in MGM's Culver City Studios.

Avena's efforts to medievalize the city began in the mid-1920s, with a radical transformation of Castelvecchio, a fortified residence built just after 1350 by Verona's ruling lord, Cangrande II della Scala. Avena also put his distinctive touch on the della Scala-era Palazzo della Provincia, in Piazza dei Signori, reopening the ground-floor gallery and crowning the restored facade with battlements, a dramatic retroaddition to the square where a towering statue of Dante has stood since 1865.

Dante in Verona

Come and behold Montecchi and Cappelletti,
Monaldi and Fillippeschi, careless man!
Those sad already, and these doubt-depressed!
Canto VI, Purgatory, The Divine Comedy

Veronese politics during Dante's time (1265–1321) echoed the furious tug-of-war between church and state that was happening over most of Europe. And Dante was in the thick of it. Accused of political corruption and exiled for life from his native Florence, where as a leader of the Whites, the faction of the Guelph party that insisted the city be free of papal control, he made his way to Verona. This was in 1303, around the time that Luigi da Porto, writing more than two centuries later, would set his *Newly Discovered Story of Two Noble Lovers.*

There, as a guest of the benevolent Bartolomeo della Scala, Dante found refuge and presumably learned of the four warring families mentioned in his canto. While Verona was a relatively peaceful place during Bartolomeo's brief reign, a century earlier the Guelphs, at that time a party united in support of the papacy and led locally by Count Sambonifacio of nearby San Bonifacio, were engaged in an intense blood feud with the pro-imperial Ghibellines, headed by the Montecchis. No records of the Cappellettis can be found in historical documents relative to Verona (their presence is confirmed in Cremona), but a dal Cappello family did exist and was closely tied to the San Bonifacio camp, making them enemies of the Montecchis by extension. (The Ghibelline Filippeschi and Guelph Monaldeschi families clashed in the town of Orvieto, from which the Filippeschi clan was eventually banished.)

Ultimately, in 1320, the Montecchi family was expelled from Verona for participating in a plot against Bartolomeo's more famous younger brother and successor, Cangrande I, the enlightened patron to whom Dante dedicated *Paradiso*, the final part of his *Divine Comedy*.

But it was the monuments directly connected to "Romeo and Juliet" that gave Avena the opportunity to fully exercise his vision. He knew that with a little imagination, and substantial funding, he could transform the tomb site to better suit the legend. He replaced the deteriorated access road with a formal gravel-strewn entrance leading from Via del Pontiere (once the Via del Corso) through a graceful vine-covered arbor and into the cloister.

He moved the tomb into a two-room subterranean "Shakespearean crypt," where he constructed an unabashedly theatrical setting for the vagabond relic, complete with false tombstones embedded in the pavement, a double-arched Gothic window, and as a finishing touch, an antique oil lamp.

Finally, he transferred the cherished bust of Shakespeare from the garden to the portico near the underground site and installed a plaque near the entrance inscribed with these astonishing lines:

"A GRAVE? O, NO; A LANTERN . . . .
FOR HERE LIES JVLIET, AND HER BEAVTY MAKES
THIS VAVLT A FEASTING PRESENCE, FVLL OF LIGHT."

"VNA TOMBA? OH! NO, VN FARO . . . .
PERCHE' QVI GIACE GIVLIETTA E LA SVA BELLEZZA
ILLVMINA QVESTA CRIPTA DI ETEREA LVCE.„

(SHAKESPEARE, "ROMEO AND JVLIET", ATTO V, SCENA III)

The unadorned sarcophagus, its identity so hotly debated over the centuries, finally had a worthy home.

No one could have predicted that just a few years later, during World War II, the Germans would commandeer the crypt for a radio control station. Or that it would be used as a bomb shelter during the repeated incursions that hammered the city and severely damaged the church and many surrounding buildings. The tomb again escaped destruction, and once peace was declared visitors returned in record numbers.

VISITORS LISTENING TO THE ROMEO AND JULIET
LEGEND IN THE CLOISTER OF JULIET'S TOMB, 1950S

Letters to Juliet

Potions

Take thou this vial, being then in bed,
And this distilling liquor drink thou off;
When presently through all thy veins shall run
A cold and drowsy humour, for no pulse
Shall keep his native progress, but surcease:
No warmth, no breath shall testify thou livest,
The roses in thy lips and cheeks shall fade
To wanny ashes, thy eyes' windows fall
Like death when he shuts up the day of life.
Each part, depriv'd of supple government
Shall stiff and stark and cold appear, like death,
And in this borrow'd likeness of shrunk death
Thou shalt continue two and forty hours
And then awake as from a pleasant sleep.

FRIAR LAURENCE, ACT IV, SCENE I

Like many of his fellow citizens, rich and poor, Shakespeare's Friar Laurence was an accomplished gardener, tending a plot abundant with produce, herbs, and flowers. He was expert in the healing arts as well, and used his many varieties of plants as a living pharmacy, from which he concocted a dazzling assortment of infusions, teas, lotions, ointments, and poultices for all sorts of ailments and complaints, from the utterly banal to the most perplexing matters of the heart and mind.

To alleviate the excruciating pain of a throbbing tooth, he might offer the sufferer a piece of yarrow root to gnaw on. For headache he often reached for the fernlike polypody. After thoroughly cleaning and gently simmering the plant in vinegar, he would massage the warm pulp on the poor soul's head. To improve eyesight the good friar might have the patient drink wine infused with the leaves of the delicate rue. He was confident that common maidenhair blended with oil and rubbed on the head would halt hair loss. He might give someone threatened by snakes a bundle of globe thistle to wear around the neck. And he was certain that dried asparagus root ministered with sips of well water (which was then sprinkled on the body for good measure) could vanquish the effects of a malicious spell.

So what was in the potion that he cooked up for Juliet? Certainly nothing from his garden, despite its potent harvest (or for that matter from the local apothecary's cupboards) was powerful enough to induce, then sustain, the deepest possible sleep for "two and forty hours" with virtually no aftereffects. The brew as described falls into the realm of fantasy, introduced to fulfill the needs of the plot.

Yet it's possible that Shakespeare thought such a potion existed. He certainly knew about the narcotic effects of opium and mandrake, the roots of which have a humanoid shape and, supposedly, if yanked from the ground let out a terrifying scream. Frightened of what she'll face when she wakes in the tomb, Juliet imagines, among other horrors,

> . . . shrieks like mandrakes torn out of the earth,
> That living mortals, hearing them, run mad . . .

Friar Laurence and Juliet (OIL ON CANVAS), JOHN PETTIE, EARLY 1870S

Shakespeare may have been familiar with *The Herball, or generall historie of plantes*, a massive 1597 tome by Elizabethan herbalist John Gerard, who wrote of the deathlike sleep brought on by deadly nightshade, also known as belladonna: "This kind of Nightshade causeth sleep, troubleth the mind . . . it bringeth such as have eaten thereof into a dead sleepe wherein many have died."

It's possible that Shakespeare came across a decidedly unorthodox insomnia cure devised by Andres Laguna, physician to Pope Julius III. In 1545, nineteen years before Shakespeare's birth, Laguna described watching as witches "anointed themselves" with "a certain green unguent . . . composed of herbs . . . hemlock, nightshade, henbane, and mandrake. I managed to obtain a good canister-full, which I used to anoint from head-to-toe the wife of the hangman (as a remedy for her insomnia). On being anointed, she suddenly slept such a profound sleep, with her eyes open like a rabbit (she also fittingly looked like a boiled hare), that I could not imagine how to wake her." Finally, thirty-six hours later, she woke and shouted, "Why do you wake me at such an inopportune time? I was surrounded by all the pleasure and delights of the world!"

NURSE: *Doth not rosemary and Romeo begin both with a letter?*

ROMEO: *Ay, nurse, what of that? Both with an "R."*

NURSE: *Ah. mocker! That's the dog's name, "R" is for the*
—No, I know it begins with some other letter; and she hath the
prettiest sententious of it, of you and rosemary, that it would do you
good to hear it.

Prized by Friar Laurence and his ilk as a blood purifier, baldness remedy, and, among many other medicinal uses, sooth-ing tonic for stomach upset, rosemary also possessed potent symbolic attributes. It signified new beginnings. Brides carried rosemary-studded bouquets to express their devotion. Newlyweds gave gold-dipped rosemary leaves to guests as tokens of remembrance, then retired to a mar-riage bed strewn with the fragrant herb. It kept wickedness in check and, when fashioned into a wreath, repelled evil. Finally, as expressed by a sorrowful Friar  Laurence at the funeral of Romeo and Juliet ("Dry up your tears, and stick your rosemary / On this fair corse"), it played an integral role in endings.

Dear Juliet,

*Who knows if you have ever written the word "Amore"
on a blank sheet of paper, just to look at it, without any
particular reason? I have: those five letters fill the page. I
am in love! There, I've said it all, but it's not enough. . . .
Each person will write to tell you of their feelings in
a different way, because each of us is different. Yet, if
you look closely, you will see the same luminous, happy
expression that unites all of those in love.*

          Gina R., Brescia, Italy

Dear Juliet,

*I live on the third floor. My parents don't allow my boyfriend
to come to my house. So I have to sneak him in. But it's very
difficult. Can you tell me how Romeo got to visit you? Tell
me his technique for climbing up to your room!*

  Thanks, kisses,

        Cari V., Lausanne, Switzerland

Dear Juliet,

*I am married to a charming man who blankets me with
gifts and looks after me splendidly. But the problem is,*

I don't love him. I was young when I got married and didn't know what I was doing. I had a child with him, whom I love more than anything in the world, and I don't want to lose her by leaving my husband for Eric, my lover. Juliet, advise me: should I choose stability with my husband and daughter, or happiness with my lover?

Jeanne C., ARLES, FRANCE

Dear Juliet,
My problem is very complicated and difficult. I am in love with a missionary nun. We were classmates in a course for social welfare assistants and saw each other often that year, at lunch break. A few times we even went together to the church dance. Then she left for India, where she stayed for twelve years. Now she is back in the States, working here. I am a widower, now sixty-two. I declared my love to her, but she told me she will never leave the church. She is the most beautiful, intelligent woman I've ever known. How can I convince her that with me she would have a marvelous life?
   Thank you,

Jack G., TAMPA, FLORIDA

CHAPTER THREE

The Letters Begin

❧

It turns out that Avena was not laboring alone. Ettore Solimani, the recently hired municipal custodian, was on the scene and destined to earn his own chapter in the story's elaborate history. Dressed in the standard-issue steel-gray jacket and pants and peaked cap, the middle-aged caretaker must have seemed unassuming enough. But the opposite was true. Solimani was not content to go about his duties a mere witness to the site's transformation. A firm believer in the legend, he soon added his own touches to the medievalizing process.

His work at the tomb site fit perfectly into a larger plan. After years of personal difficulties and three tours of active service—in the Libyan conflict, in World War I, and, later, a voluntary year in the Abyssinian war—Solimani, thinking of his family's future stabil-ity, was anxious for a change. He had worked on and off over the years as a photographer and chauffeur, and when he returned from

ETTORE SOLIMANI REPLYING TO JULIET'S MAIL

Africa had brief employment with the local Education Authority, a steady job that he found dull.

Life became considerably more exciting when a close friend heard that a search was on for a custodian for the run-down site. "Another would have put his mind to rest and ignored new adventures," he wrote in a series of 1958 articles for Italy's *Oggi* magazine. "But quiet and routine are not part of my character and destiny had decided that I was near to the great turning point of my existence. The best, freshest part of my life seemed over to me and I couldn't have imagined that true youth would have arrived for me only then, when I would meet Juliet, the woman of my dreams." Solimani had found his calling.

"At the time," he continues, "the Prefect of Verona was Dr. Vaccari, whose wife, Signora Juccia, took some friends to visit the tomb. She found it abandoned, without a guard, dirty, neglected, as though Verona rejected the honor of having given birth to the most famous heroine of love of all time. The next day, Signora Vaccari called to report the matter to the podesta [mayor], who was the lawyer Alberto Donella. Donella and the vice-podesta decided right away to act and guarantee Juliet a better arrangement and a custodian. A dear friend of mine knew they were looking for the right man and mentioned my name. I was summoned to the municipal building and asked, explicitly, if I would accept the job. The fact is that I thought it over a bit and, as was my habit, decided to trust in the spirit of adventure that even at forty-six years of age didn't cease to inspire me.

Letters to Juliet

"It was April 12, 1937. I remember it as if it were today. In the office of the municipal vice-secretary, in the presence of the then-director of the Verona art museums, I was given the keys to the entrance gate and the block of tickets for the entrance fee. They began exactly with the number 63.111. From that moment, I was the custodian of the tomb. Juliet, modestly, had found her secretary."

Propelled by his dedication to the myth, and deeply dissatisfied with what he felt was the city's inadequate attention to the site, Solimani made it his mission to give Juliet her due. He understood that, though the visitors who arrived in ever-increasing numbers knew the basic story, they were after something more, something extraordinary to make them feel part of the legend.

SOUVENIR PIN DESIGNED BY ETTORE SOLIMANI INSCRIBED WITH THE PHRASE *Se ami credi in Giuletta* (*If you love, believe in Juliet*)

It may have helped that along with the keys to the gate, the city gave Solimani use of an apartment for himself and his family, just across the cloister from the tomb. At his own expense he planted some forty rosebushes in the central garden and, near the entrance to the crypt, a large weeping willow tree. He bought and trained two dozen snow-white turtledoves to circle the cloister and land, on cue, on the shoulders of delighted female visitors.

TOURISTS PERFORMING THE "RITUAL OF LOVE" WITH ETTORE SOLIMANI LOOKING ON, 1940S

Solimani's involvement didn't stop there. An indefatigable show‑ man, he understood the pull of the myth and the desire for some sort of "direct contact" with Juliet. One thing led to many others, and it wasn't long before Solimani had devised the fanciful "ritual of love," of which he was director and cameraman. He invited couples, married and not, to follow him into the crypt and to stand one on either side of the tomb. Hold hands, he would say, and think of a *pensiero d'amore* (love thought) and exchange a kiss. He told them that Juliet would surely make their wish come true, and from that moment on they were under the idealized protection of love's greatest heroine.

Solimani later recalled an oddly formal young couple who visited the site and, after completing the ritual of love, asked him if they could leave a letter for Juliet, in her tomb. Of course he said yes.

We, two newlyweds, having by the grace of God been able to realize our love, united in life, remembering you always, kneel now at the foot of your sacred tomb, the destination of lovers from all over the world, where you, Juliet, met your tragic end along with your Romeo. We write this to remember you in life and to tell you that we pray for your eternal peace.

Before long tourists began to leave ornate calling cards behind, many covered with hastily scribbled messages that recalled the earliest notes left for Juliet around the turn of the century. Some slipped more effusive sentiments into the glass-fronted niche near the staircase leading to the crypt—Juliet's first mailbox.

Still others recorded spontaneous thoughts next to their signatures in the guestbook that Solimani strategically placed on a large stand at the tomb's entrance. "In perpetual memory of the antique lovers, we dream of love, eternally," wrote an Italian soldier in 1943. Sharing the page are signatures of tourists from Padua, Rome, Milan, and Brescia, as well as Belgium. Solimani encouraged everyone to sign, a wonderfully democratic gesture that merged autographs and comments by Ginger Rogers, Greta Garbo, Vivien Leigh, Laurence Olivier, Maria Callas, Andrey Gromyko, and the duke of Windsor, among many other luminaries, with those of the general public. The wife of Giovanni Gronchi, then Italy's president, was so impressed by Solimani's endeavors that she arranged for him to be named a cavalier of the republic.

Not all messages were composed on the spot. Letters began arriving from far away, from writers inspired by articles about the City of Lovers and the wildly popular Cukor film. Addressed simply "Giulietta, Verona," or, sometimes, "Juliet, Verona," these missives began to accumulate at the tomb site.

They certainly couldn't languish. So Solimani, true to form, slipped into character and began replying, in order to "calm that too-rough sea and console some who weep uncontrollably." He devoted his evenings to this task, composing every letter on an old typewriter in his apartment and financing the postage with his tips. It helped that during his war years he had picked up a smattering of English and French. Thanks to his diligent, remarkably candid replies, some writers eventually addressed their mail directly to Solimani or, rather, to "the Secretary of Juliet."

67 16 Aprile 1943

Gustavia de Lota

Vuonen Porto 6   Brescia

[illegible]

16-4-43 Milano

19 Aprile 1943 XXI

17 Aprile 43 XXI

His role was established and there was no turning back. The letters kept on coming and Solimani continued to respond. When assuming the voice of Juliet's loyal secretary, he was a pragmatic shoot-from-the-hip counselor, and though he treated each letter with tact and compassion, he could occasionally be quite stern, even chiding, when he felt a writer had behaved badly. His responses were also often undeniably quaint, especially when advising women about their marital responsibilities.

Dear Juliet,

For more than five years I have fought to overcome my pain, yet have found neither comfort nor relief. No one but you, I suppose, can understand how much power the heart's passion holds. I lost my love and my husband to another, who, with cunning and wickedness, inventing shameful lies about me, stole him from me. Because of my pride, and even more so because of the pain, I was unable to defend myself or even fight to recapture my love. For ten years he was everything to me, in spite of endless obstacles that continually blocked our path. Neither the war, nor his time in prison, our poverty, his obligation to support his elderly parents, or two operations had been able to shatter our love.

But an intruder succeeded, damning us both. Him, because he returned to the road of perdition, from which I, with much patience and sacrifice, had saved him, making him an honest man. Me, because I have moments of folly and am afraid I will not be able to overcome the desperateness of this battle. Juliet, I am putting myself in your compassionate hands because I am alone in the world, without help, protection, or sage advice. I put my hope in you because you are the protector of all pure hearts that suffer. Help me! Save me! I feel suspended on a precipice. I am afraid of going mad. I can no longer cry because my eyes are tired and weak. Excuse me for my ranting, but I couldn't help telling you the secret of my unhappy love. I don't have the means to visit your tomb, but just the same do something so that my Vincenzo, my only reason for living, returns to me with the love we once had.

A.L., Treviso, Italy

Dearest Lady,

Juliet received your letter and I am taking the liberty of replying, as I am the custodian of her tomb and of her legend. Madam, you believe blindly in the power of Juliet's love, but if tomorrow you realize that it is only an illusion, imagine what a sad shock you would have! You ask for advice that is difficult to give: a woman has come between you and your husband, but I say to you with all my heart that one must never despair.

Do you believe, sincerely, that your husband understood you? Do you think you understood him and the complexities of his character? Men have moments when they are unable to control themselves, when they don't know where to go. They feel that family life is dull, they want a change, and, finding she who seconds these feelings, they throw themselves into these false temptations. Yet how dearly they always pay for this mistake and how strongly they desire, later, to go back and to be forgiven! You know that when a woman wants to she can overcome all obstacles, because only she knows all the secrets of her man, how to handle him, and how to keep him.

Madam, I have no power to convince your husband to return to you, but the suggestion I make to people who write to me about situations like yours is to have faith, to persevere, and to not become discouraged. The day of humiliation will come for the intruder, and your husband will come back to you, remorseful for the pain he caused you. In marriage I have been happy, but I know this also has its thorns. For this reason I say that a woman must not just think of herself as the wife of her husband, but also as his advisor, sister, friend, and even mother.

Were you all of these things? If yes, your man will look for you again, have no fear! I will end here, dear lady. Do not give up hope. Remember that life is a continual battle, and that the body wears down but the spirit remains and that love triumphs, always. Continue to believe in Juliet, who from her sky of love will guide and protect you.

Not all correspondents were women:

Dear Custodian of Juliet's Tomb,
Can you bring a word of peace and comfort to my wounded heart? I have a wife and two children, three creatures from Paradise. We were happy until another woman appeared in my life, a woman with the same blood as my wife. I love her and she loves me desperately. Do you understand, Juliet, the enormity of this situation? We feel we can no longer resist, that we are at the breaking point. Save me, save me, save me!

Rudolfo

Dear Sir,

*I am the custodian of Juliet's tomb, but I am not a
man who can perform miracles. I must confess that
in all the years I have been doing this, I've never come
across a request like yours. Where can I find a word of
comfort for you? How did you get into this situation?
You must remember you have a serious responsibility:
a wife and children. Have you never thought that your
current situation is unconscionable in that you could
be accused of lacking respect for your own dignity? Sir,
at your age you must use reason. Even the strongest
passions can be commandeered and overcome. Have
you never thought what your reaction would be if your
wife were to fall in love with one of your brothers?*

*Pull yourself together, I beg you, and face your
responsibilities as husband and father. Rebuild peace in
your family. Tell the "other" that your encounter was
only a moment of weakness and that you must both
forget it. Believe me, Juliet cannot offer any more than
suggestions in a case like yours, because her love for
Romeo does not belong to the category of sinful loves. I
hope that these words bring you some comfort, as though
from a father.*

Dear Far-Away Friend,

I read a magazine article about you and was captivated. What you do is so wonderful and romantic! You must truly be a marvelous person. I would like to meet you and talk to you, but that is impossible. I have been married for many years, but not happily. I am agitated and nervous and I don't really feel like I'm married. I ardently desire reciprocated love and friendship, yet I feel guilty for having these thoughts. I hope for some miracle or that something else will happen to take me out of this situation. I wish happiness for everyone; I wish for my husband to be happy, even if I am not happy with him. What should I do? I know you are very busy, but please find the time to reply to me. Do you think that the power of love can work, even for me? I hope you won't think I am a foolish woman. I wish you health and happiness. Please, write to me. I've never been photogenic, but I am including a picture of me taken last winter in the snow.

Your Catherine, LANSING, MICHIGAN, 1950

Dear Lady,

In your message, you tell me that you are not happy with your husband. Life between a husband and wife is not as easy as it might seem in the first days of a marriage. One cannot expect to always feel in love like at the first instant, even if the task of keeping the flame alive falls to the woman. Yet we in Italy consider love the purpose of life and for this reason we teach our women that love knows no obstacles, but leads to a life of complete happiness.

You should also know, dear lady, that the greatest responsibility for this happiness depends on the woman, because she must understand the love of her husband in all its purity, considering it the sole purpose of her existence. Thus it must be you who takes the first step toward reconciliation, who supports, tolerates, and makes the peace. The most sincere wishes to you, from he who guards the site of the tragedy of Romeo and Juliet with love and, in the name of their great sacrifice, wishes that you might find that happiness that the two young Veronese lovers surely found in Heaven.

Some of these early letters address Juliet with veneration. This one,
from France:

> Dear Juliet,
> I am turning to you with faith, as though to a saint. I
> am falling in love with a young man who is courting me,
> but I'm afraid he may be too high-class for me. Lucien is
> a surveyor, and so elegant and handsome. He is twenty-
> five. How can he love a poor seamstress of seventeen?
> I hope with all my heart that he is sincere and that he
> will ask me to marry him. I would love him, I feel it, for
> all my life. Juliet, it is for this reason that I write to you
> from so far away, hoping you can help me. Hear me,
> please, hear me, and if it is indeed as I hope I will come
> to see you with my Lucien.

And from a heartsick young man:

> You are so beautiful, Juliet, and so on high, yet all hearts
> in love look to you and speak to you. Those who are in
> love and who suffer in love look to you. I know many
> write to you and I do as well, because I believe in you,
> Juliet, and I turn to you as I did when, as a humble sol-
> dier, I came to see you during the war. Now the war is
> over, but I am poor, Juliet, and she is not. When I speak
> to her, you are there too, Juliet, listening to me and giving

*me courage. My mind tells me not to love her because I
cannot compare myself to her, but my heart pushes me
ahead, in spite of all the obstacles. I know you did not
listen to the voice of the mind, either. Whoever, for you,
reads this letter, help me!*

Ludovico N.

Looking back on his twenty-odd years as secretary to Juliet and guardian of her tomb, Solimani had this to say: "Among the thousands of letters that arrived addressed to Juliet, along with the truly moving were some really insipid ones written by stupid little girls infatuated with older boys, who begged for a glance from him, as though they were talking about some divinity! I kept and catalogued these and sometimes replied paternally. Two smacks would have been a better cure, however, in certain cases."

In 1958 Ettore Solimani reached the state-imposed retirement age of sixty-seven and was forced to leave his post. His unhappiness was mollified, somewhat, when in a truly gratifying reversal of roles, he began to receive letters of support from thankful correspondents as well as from those who had read of his undertaking.

Dear Cavaliere Solimani,

I am an elementary school teacher in a small town
in Texas, land of cowboys and the Far West. The sad
story of Romeo and Juliet has moved me since I was a
child, and when I visited Italy some years ago my first
desire was to see Juliet's tomb. You showed me around,
telling me many details that only Juliet's secretary could
know. Now, opening my newspaper, I see that you have
reached the "age limit" after which one must retire. This
news will surely make many foreign tourists who have
visited Verona sad, knowing that when they return to
the "temple of love" they will no longer be greeted by the
REAL secretary, but by a substitute nobody without any
merit or qualifications.

The Veronese Authorities haven't considered a very
important detail: as the legend of the unhappy lovers
has lasted through the centuries, so Juliet's secretary can
never reach an "age limit" because the Love Story, like
its characters, never grows old. Don't take it too much
to heart, Cav. Solimani, if the authorities with their
cold bureaucratic mentality have carried out a purely
administrative act. For all of us, the American tourists,
for all those who passionately admire this great tragedy
that made Verona famous, you, and only you, will always
be the true Secretary of Juliet.

William W.

Solimani was fully aware of his impact and, though he never completed the manuscript, he developed an outline for a book. He shared his plans with the Italian journalist Piero Marcolini, who wrote in the newspaper *Il Corriere di Trieste* that Solimani, "encouraged by influential people," had decided to write a memoir filled with "twenty years of impressions and experiences as the most poetic custodian in the world." According to Marcolini, Solimani had "drafted pages and pages" and mapped out the following chapters:

❖ EXPERIENCES AS SECRETARY
❖ CONSIDERATIONS ON LOVE
❖ LETTERS AND ADVICE TO MARRIED WOMEN
❖ TO YOUNG WOMEN
❖ TO FOREIGNERS (LISTING THE COUNTRIES IN ALPHABETICAL ORDER)
❖ THE MOST GENTLE SOULS LOVE JULIET

Marcolini wrote that the "most central chapter will without doubt be devoted to the correspondence," and that "the author intends to call the book 'Juliet Capulet and Solimani, her Guardian.'"

"I love Juliet," Solimani confided to Marcolini at the time, "not like Romeo, but better."

Toward the end of his life, Solimani philosophically summed up his two decades at the tomb: "I always did my duty as custodian, trying to make the best use, to my city's advantage, of the modern myth that—after the antique, immortal one—had surrounded the figure of the most famous young lady of Verona, Juliet."

CHAPTER FOUR

Juliet's House... and Romeo's

✦

While most Juliet-related activities during the Solimani era occurred at or around the tomb, her presence was never confined to the site. As early as the mid-1800s, locals identified her house as a run-down, five-story brick building on the present-day Via Cappello. Like many surviving buildings with portions dating to medieval times, various owners added structural elements piecemeal over the centuries, resulting in the eclectic three-sided complex that is visible today. The tower section, a defensive edifice facing the street, suggests the residents' affiliation with a powerful political faction.

Early on, the house served as an informal inn for travelers, and probably sheltered their horses as well. Somewhat later, part of the building was relegated to small shops that continued in some form

JULIET'S HOUSE (WITH VAULTED ENTRANCE), C. 1910

or other as the property passed through many hands. The Cappelletti family that Dante refers to in *The Divine Comedy* never lived in Verona. But a dal Cappello clan did, and an endless stream of multilingual tour guides points to the bonnet-like hat carved in the courtyard vault's keystone as proof of the family's ties to the house.

Less romantic observers suggest that at one time a hatmaker may have set up shop here. (*Cappello* means "hat" in Italian.) Whether the name Cappelletti (in Shakespeare, Capulet) is simply a phonetic distortion of dal Cappello remains open to debate. Whatever the truth, the site has attracted the curious, and opinionated, for nearly two centuries.

When Charles Dickens paid a visit on his way to the tomb in 1844, he paused in the courtyard and declared the house had "degenerated into a most miserable inn." His unsparing description of the scene continues:

> Noisy vetturini and muddy market-carts were disputing possession of the yard, which was ankle-deep in dirt, with a brood of splashed and bespattered geese; and there was a grim-visaged dog, viciously panting in a doorway, who would certainly have had Romeo by the leg, the moment he put it over the wall, if he had existed and been at large in those times.

Things hadn't improved much in 1868, when American author and critic William Dean Howells recorded his impressions in *Italian Journeys*.

COURTYARD OF JULIET'S HOUSE, EARLY 1900S

We found it a very old and time-worn edifice, built round an ample court, and we knew it, as we had been told we should, by the cap carved in stone above the interior of the grand portal. The family, anciently one of the principal in Verona, has fallen from much of its former greatness . . . There was a great deal of stable litter, and many empty carts standing about in the court, and if I might hazard the opinion formed upon these and other appearances, I should say that old Capulet has now gone to keeping a hotel, united with the retail liquor business, both in a small way.

About twenty years later, American writer E. D. R. Bianciardi wrote about his honeymoon visit for *Harper's New Monthly Magazine.*

The palace where the noble of Verona once feasted his friends, was now a tavern of the humblest sort, where refreshments for man and beast were sold, not given. And, as if this was not enough to destroy the charm . . . there depended long lines of wet garments of every shape and hue, and a vile-tongued parrot screaming at us from his perch.

In 1905, when a part of the house complex was finally put up for sale at auction, a sentimental public pressured the Comune di Verona to place the winning bid of 7500 lire, equal to approximately €27,000.00, or about $31,000, an absurdly low figure by today's standards. The city purchased the wing that runs along the right side of the courtyard and three floors of the side facing the street, a section noted in 1914 by the Superintendency of Cultural Heritage as being of architectural interest. But due to the Great War and post-conflict priorities to renew the city's urban fabric, "Juliet's house," as it was now known, remained in abject condition until around 1940, when Antonio Avena decided to create a monument equal to the sites so brilliantly (if fantastically) rendered in Cukor's recently released movie. Avena had already realized his vision at the tomb site, converting the ramshackle entrance into a picturesque walkway, and designing an appropriately Shakespearean setting for the much abused sepulchral. The house required a more radical facelift.

Avena enlivened the sober courtyard facade with recycled architectural elements. He arranged the installation of a rose window, a Gothic portal, several trefoil window frames recovered from previously demolished antique buildings, and, his most ingenious addition, a balcony pieced together from a carved marble slab (in its original incarnation probably one side of a fourteenth-century sarcophagus) and two unrelated side elements from the same period.

Though unlike the curved balcony in Cukor's hit, which was modeled after Donatello's exterior pulpit for the Duomo in Prato, Avena's boxier version enchanted visitors from the moment it was unveiled, and continues to lure them upstairs today, to stand where "she" stood and so famously called, "O Romeo, Romeo! Wherefore art thou Romeo?" (Avena initially had hoped to make the house a permanent home to the hundreds of sketches, costumes, photographs, and set pieces associated with the Cukor film. He eventually did negotiate an exhibition at the Castelvecchio Museum, but once it ended nothing remained in the city.)

Avena made few structural changes inside the house itself. He instead focused his energy and imagination on the construction of a series of scenographic rooms inspired by pictorial sources. The first-floor salon is an uncanny re-creation of the decor in *L' addio di Romeo a Giulietta* by the popular Italian Romantic painter Francesco Hayez (see page 14).

Avena also borrowed liberally from local monuments. The keel-shaped wooden ceiling in the church of San Fermo is reproduced on a much smaller scale on the house's uppermost story—here, punctuated by stars rather than saints—as are colorful decorative elements Avena uncovered during his revamping of Castelvecchio.

Decades later, in the 1970s, workers revamped the interior spaces, staircases, and floors, and the Lion's Club donated a bronze sculpture of a pensive Juliet by the late Veronese sculptor Nereo Costantini. She stands in the courtyard, just steps from the front door of her house. (Full-size casts of the Costantini work also embellish Munich's Mareinplatz and the plaza fronting Chicago's Shakespeare Theater.)

In the 1990s the rooms were refurbished with antique furniture, an assortment of paintings related to the story (among them Veronese painter Angelo Dall'Oca Bianca's *The Death of Romeo and Juliet*), and detached frescoes transplanted from various local buildings.

What ho! No balcony!

Although the balcony is surely the most vivid architectural element in our collective images of Shakespeare's *Romeo and Juliet,* the playwright never actually mentions one. In the second scene of Act II, Juliet is described as entering from "above," eliciting Romeo's indelible lines:

> *But soft, what light through yonder window breaks?*
> *It is the east and Juliet is the sun!*

Juliet reenters twice, in the same scene, and always from "above." That Shakespeare doesn't specify a balcony in his playscript may stem from the fact that Elizabethan theaters were routinely constructed with balconies, or boxes, as onstage architectural elements, and he may have felt that his direction was sufficient to indicate that one should be used in the famous scene.

SCENE FROM ACT II, PERFORMED AT THE THEATRE NATIONAL DE L'OPERA, 1888 (ENGRAVING), PAUL DESTEZ

Even though Luigi da Porto's *A Newly Discovered Story of Two Noble Lovers* is the only version among the story's direct literary antecedents to make an overt reference to a balcony, there's no question that it has worked wonderfully as a dramatic device since at least the mid-eighteenth century. There have been exceptions, of course. One of the more outré occurs in Baz Luhrmann's 1996 film *Romeo + Juliet*. The director set the scene in a swimming pool, underscoring the recurring watery imagery that binds the lovers.

Baci di Giulietta

In the late 1940s, another Veronese put his talents at the service of the legend. Enzo Perlini's story begins in the 1920s, when his father founded Verona's first Pasticceria Perlini. Young Enzo grew up in the bakery's kitchen, along with two brothers and a sister, who worked up front. When they became adults, each sibling set up shop (at one point there were five in town), and just after the war Enzo established his own, on Via Cappello, facing the Casa di Giulietta.

By this time Juliet's house was attracting an increasing number of tourists, and Perlini felt the moment was right to create a pastry bearing her name. The Baci di Giulietta (Juliet's kisses) were born. An ethereal combination of beaten egg whites, sugar, hazelnuts, and cocoa, eloquently described by Perlini as "a smooth hazelnut cream-based

Enzo Perlini in front of the Pasticceria Perlini, 1987

mixture that always leaves one with the desire to enjoy another," the baci were a hit from the start. Unaware that in order to patent a recipe it had to be registered before being marketed to the public, Perlini never bothered to complete the paperwork for his formula. Though this lapse freed other pastry chefs in town to turn out their own copycat versions of the baci, his booming business was unaffected.

More than three decades later Perlini launched (and this time patented) two additional treats. He characterizes each with typical flair. The Cuori di Giulietta e Romeo (The hearts of Juliet and Romeo) symbolize "two hearts that feel joined by a sweet love that finishes on the palate with a delicate but desired bitter note," while the bittersweet chocolate Sorrisi di Romeo (Romeo's smiles) are evidently dangerous, "filled with a rum flavored cream—not too alcoholic but enough so to make one say, 'Yes!' to Juliet."

Though the consummate artistry of the finished product may be slightly beyond most home cooks, the essence of the baci—the taste, texture, and aroma—will reward those who have a little patience and the courage to wield a pastry bag.

BACI DI GIULIETTA

For the cookies

1½ cups (½ pound) hazelnuts, blanched, peeled, and toasted

¾ cup granulated sugar

2½ tablespoons unsweetened cocoa powder (best quality)

4 large egg whites

For the filling

8 tablespoons margarine (butter becomes too soft)

¾ cup powdered sugar

1 teaspoon rum, cognac or Grand Marnier

¼ cup unsweetened cocoa powder

1½ ounce bittersweet chocolate, melted and cooled (this helps solidify the mixture)

To make the cookies, combine the hazelnuts with ¼ cup of the sugar in the bowl of a food processor. Pulse on and off until the nuts are ground to a fine powder (processing continuously will cause the mixture to become oily). Transfer to a bowl and stir in the cocoa powder.

In the bowl of a standing electric mixer, beat the egg whites on medium speed until frothy. Increase the speed to high and gradually add the remaining sugar. Beat the whites until glossy and stiff (but not dry).

Gradually fold the nut mixture into the whites, turning the bowl as you go. Work slowly and gently to keep the whites firm.

Line several cookie sheets with parchment paper. Alternatively, use non-stick cookie sheets.

Fit a pastry bag with a ¼-inch-wide star tip. Working with half the batter at a time, gently fill the bag. Hold the bag vertically about two inches from the cookie sheet and pipe out forms that are slightly bigger than a quarter (the batter must fall from the tip and not be pressed against the sheet). Pipe out one at a time, 1½ inches apart, moving on to the next with a flipping motion that leaves lines in the dough. Makes about 80 small cookies. Set aside and let rest, uncovered and undisturbed, for 24 hours at room temperature.

Preheat the oven to 250° F. Working two sheets at a time, bake the baci until slightly firm to the touch, about 10 minutes. Remove and completely cool on the sheets. Loosen carefully with a spatula and set aside.

To prepare the filling, combine the margarine and powdered sugar in the bowl of a standing electric mixer. Beat on low speed until smooth. Add the rum, cocoa powder, and melted chocolate. Mix until blended. (Makes about 1 cup filling.)

Use a pastry bag or small spoon to put a dot of filling—about 1 teaspoon—on the sides of half the cookies. Add another cookie to each and gently press to adhere. Set aside at room temperature until the filling has solidified, about an hour. Makes about 40 baci.

ROMEO'S HOUSE, ALSO KNOWN AS CASA NOGAROLA, IN THE 1920S

It's just a brief stroll from Juliet's house to Romeo's—a two-minute sprint across what were, in 1303, botanical gardens, and the young Montague would have been at his true love's balcony. These days, surprisingly few tourists find their way here. Those who do make the detour are rewarded with a glimpse at one of the most authentic medieval structures in the city.

But they can't get inside. The fortress-like palazzo on Via delle Arche identified as Romeo's house is now in private hands, making it the most elusive of all the sites tied to the myth. Visitors are limited to admiring the architecture and scrutinizing the marble plaque on its facade.

O, WHERE IS ROMEO ? . . . .
. . . .
TVT, I HAVE LOST MYSELF; I AM NOT HERE;
THIS IS NOT ROMEO, HE'S SOME OTHER WHERE.

OH! DOV'E' ROMEO ? . . . .
. . . .
TACI; HO PERDVTO ME STESSO; IO NON SON QVI
E NON SON ROMEO; ROMEO E' ALTROVE.

(DA SHAKESPEARE, "ROMEO AND JVLIET", ATTO I, SCENA I)

Whoever selected these passages seems to have questioned the presumed connection to Shakespeare's hero.

The austere brick building with its imposing, battle-ready walls dates at least in part to the della Scala dynasty. In his *Memorie storiche*, the sixteenth-century Veronese historian Jacopo Rizzoni mentions the fallout of a violent feud between rival factions in 1206 that led to the destruction of the "Monticoli house, near Ponte Nuovo," a reference that convinced many observers to take a leap of faith. The powerful Montecchis almost certainly lived in the immediate area, but proof of their possession of this complex is pretty scant. On the other hand, there are documents detailing the house's lineage during the fourteenth and fifteenth centuries. Among its most illustrious residents were the Nogarola family, close allies of the della Scalas. (The Veronese refer to the building as both Casa Nogarola and Romeo's house.) After the wealthy Bevilacqua Lazise family's brief occupancy during the 1400s, various owners reconfig-ured much of the structure.

What happened next remains murky, though it's obvious that the house's noble architectural style didn't prevent its serious neglect well into the twentieth century. In her 1907 book, *The Story of Verona*, the British historian Alethea Wiel wrote, "Though it is in a dreadful state . . . the beauty of the brickwork and of different styles of arches—some round, some pointed—is very apparent."

Interest in the house was briefly rekindled around 1920, when Avena proposed that the Superintendency for Cultural Heritage use it for the literary society. The city tabled his idea and, in 1938, urged the superintendency to locate its offices as well as a new Shake-speare museum within the palazzo. This proposal didn't go anywhere either. World War II began and the building remained in a dilapidated state for several more decades.

At one point the city converted the house into a stable, a demotion that embarrassed many Veronese, who freely expressed their outrage in the local press. Guido Tombetti, the former director of the newspaper *Adige*, wrote in 1948, "What a mockery of destiny: this superb building, which at night in the light of the moon offers us at once the vision of a bellicose epoch, has become a stall."

In 1957, well before the current owners undertook a sensitive restoration, a prominent citizen wrote an editorial for the now-defunct periodical *Vita Veronese*, pleading with the city to restore the house to its original, medieval appearance and to fill it with prints, drawings, and paintings illustrating Verona's distinguished past. Using the words of the first-century B.C. Roman historian Sallust, he admonishes: "It is not shameful to possess nothing; but it is total inanity to lose what one already has." Ten years later, the magazine's founding editor, Gino Beltramini, took on a major role in the story of Juliet's correspondence.

CHAPTER FIVE

The "Prof"

Born in Verona in 1908, Gino Beltramini was an active promoter of the city's history and popular traditions and dedicated to maintaining the vitality of the local dialect. Small and wiry, with piercing blue eyes, he was for years a highly regarded high school professor whose riveting delivery—Italian peppered with a mix of Latin, Greek, and Veronese—earned him a following far beyond the classroom.

In 1948 he and two friends founded *Vita Veronese*, an eclectic monthly whose ambitious mission was to "make known to an ever-increasing public, even beyond the august provincial confines, the multiple aspects of Veronese life—glories and misadventures, men and multitudes, works, institutions and ideas." Though the magazine published articles by many fine local scholars and writers during its nearly forty-year life, it was always pitched to a general audience, to those who "love to find in reading a rest, a

GINO BELTRAMINI, 1970S

lively memory of past times, a relaxed exposition of various aspects of the present."

Because of the magazine's sweeping editorial scope, facets of the Romeo and Juliet legend were tackled repeatedly over the years, and in 1951 an entire issue was dedicated to the topic. Beltramini, signing his pen name, "Gibe," wrote the introduction, which concludes with this disclaimer:

> Perhaps some readers will say to us: enough already! With so many problems, with nimbuses on the horizon, with so many worries of every sort, don't you have anything else to worry about than a "legend"? To these few we respond that if many people distract themselves from their daily problems with an interest in sports, cinema, etc., etc., then why should we be denied the possibility to be dreamers, and once in a while be able to express and defend our illusions?

Beltramini edited *Vita Veronese* from his "office" in a corner of the Libreria Dante, a well-known bookstore, where every day after 5:00 P.M. he could be found in a corner furnished with two easy chairs and a bookshelf holding copies of every issue. From here "the prof," as he was universally known, held court, oversaw the magazine, and worked on his notable Italian-Veronese dictionary as well as other publications. It seems inevitable that when the head of Verona's tourism office was searching for someone to fill Ettore Solimani's role as secretary to Juliet he turned to Beltramini. His daughter, Silvana, recalls that he accepted the role, "motivated by a love for all that was Veronese" and a belief that the legend "opens the heart to hope."

Beltramini began responding in 1967, nine years after Solimani's retirement. During the hiatus, city officials had relegated Juliet's incoming mail to a few shelves in the tourism office. When Beltramini began his new position, all letters addressed to Juliet and, rarely, Romeo, were first translated by city employees, then delivered to the secretary. As extroverted and gregarious as he could be when in the company of colleagues or speaking in public, Beltramini was equally reserved and discreet about private affairs, and agreed to take on the role of secretary on the condition that the city maintain absolute secrecy. Only Silvana, who assisted him in the preparation of many of his publications (never the letters), and a few close friends were aware of his involvement.

"What is surprising," he told a journalist from the Milan weekly *La Settimana Radio-TV* in 1969, on strict condition of anonymity, "is the sincerity, the almost scary sincerity of these letters, in which girls and women tell of their suffering in love, spats, cruel abandonment, and complicated quarrels. I would say that these messages have the merit of a spontaneous authenticity of feelings, even when they pose extremely delicate questions, revealing an absolute absence of hypocrisy."

Beltramini replied to every letter by hand, on stationery embossed with a drawing of the now-famous balcony, and signed with a barely

decipherable "Juliet." He always answered in Italian. He felt it would have been absurd to write in a language other than the heroine's own. "If I had her reply in English or use the Cyrillic alphabet," he explained to a journalist from *Famiglia Cristiana*, in 1972, "it would no longer be Juliet. Juliet is from Verona, and it should already be considered an infringement if I use Italian. The fair-haired Capulet spoke, and wrote, in Veronese."

The hundreds of letters Beltramini replied to touch on many of the themes that occur again and again in the earlier correspondence: unrequited love, love lost, betrayal. They also reflect pressing social and political issues of the time—most strikingly, interracial relationships and the Vietnam War.

Dear Juliet,

I want to express in these small and simple words how much I need you. I am an unhappy boy, who has never loved, and I want you to give me the force to begin. You, who are the queen of hearts, help me! Dear Secretary of Juliet, how much longer must I wait?

Marco B., VARESE, ITALY, 1968

Dear Secretary of Juliet,

I have a terrible love problem. My boyfriend and I are both young adults and know what we want, but my parents forbid me to see him. They say I'm too young and may get in trouble, but this is not true. I'm a sensible girl and know the right thing to do and the right time to do it. Now my real problem is this: my boyfriend is getting tired of sitting home every night because I can't go out, and is thinking of going out with other girls. I can't let this happen, but don't know how to stop it. Please help me keep him, and FAST!

Marjorie C., Boston, Massachusetts, 1969

P.S. Please rush your advice to me before I lose my boy-friend.

❧

Dear Secretary of Juliet,

I've got a terrible problem. Five years ago I met a Negro boy, William, at Bible camp. We became friends and have kept in touch over the years. William and I are in love. We don't really mind our racial differences but everyone else does. My parents and friends are against us getting married. William and I have separated many times, trying to get over each other. But each time we realize it is no good. We don't want to get married against our parents' will but they won't see our side. We heard about you from a friend. We're desperate. Can you find any solution to our problem?

    Sincerely,

Peggy P., Bozeman, Montana, 1970

P.S. I enclosed a self-addressed envelope.

❧

Dear Juliet,
I am in love with a black man. He is good, sweet, affectionate. My parents don't want him in our house and will never consent to our marriage. Sometimes I go to his house, and we are like husband and wife. It is wonderful! Maybe we will run far away, where there is respect for feelings and for humanity. Juliet, do marvelous countries like that exist?

Maggie R., Providence, Rhode Island

Greetings, the greatest of the greats,
Immortal like love itself!
Hello, Juliet!
There are people in the world who believe in the gods, in
miracles, and there are people who don't believe, but there
is one divinity in which all seek refuge. This divinity is
Love, the most beautiful, superb sentiment in the world.

Fyodor V., LENINGRAD, USSR

꧂

Dear Mr. Secretary to Juliet,
I have this horrible problem. As Romeo with Rosaline,
I have an unrequited love. Day after day it seems to get
worse. He acts as though I am not alive. What can I do
besides forget him? I love him dearly.

Angela C., ATLANTA, GEORGIA, 1967

꧂

Dear Romeo,
I have asked the advice of your beloved Juliet and now I
would like to ask you a question. If the Montague and
Capulet families were at peace at the time you married
and your marriage continued to be happy, do you think
Juliet would have killed herself for you if you had to

leave, or would she continue to live with only happy
memories? This question, if answered, would satisfy the
curiosity my friends and I share about how strong your
love is. So please reply.

  Sincerely,

Monica W., CAMBRIDGE, ENGLAND, 1969

❧

Dear Juliet,
I am a sixteen-year-old girl, and like you I am in love.
But between us there is a small (or big) difference.
Your parents tried to stop you and didn't allow you to
love Romeo, while mine don't say anything, but there is
something that stops me. When I was ten I got polio and
four years ago had an operation that went well. I walk
almost normally, but my right leg is slightly smaller than
the left below the knee. The boy I love knows about my
illness but he doesn't know about the smaller leg. I want
to know if I should tell him or wait a little longer. He
really does love me. At times we even talk about getting
married. He is eighteen and lives in Bergamo.

  Please, Juliet, can you give me some advice?
  Thank you!

Mina S., LODI, ITALY, 1972

PS. You know, I care about you like a sister. I visited Verona and I loved your beautiful city! Ciao, Juliet!

❧

Dear Juliet,

I wrote to you many years ago and your advice helped me so much. Now that I am no longer a teenager I realize I once again need your advice. My husband, Roger, has been in the army for two years. He is fighting in Vietnam. I have since fallen in love with Roger's best friend. Although my husband and I were unhappy together, I still find myself falling more and more into a depression when I think of his return. My life is very empty now and I need someone.

Please, help me!

Andrea M., BATON ROUGE, LOUISIANA, 1967

❧

Dear Juliet,

I am in a bunker. Outside I hear missiles exploding, bullets being fired. I am twenty-two years old and I'm scared. Our commander has told us that soon we must come out. A hand-to-hand battle awaits us. I feel I will die. I leave life with this brief note. I am entrusting it to

you, symbol of universal love. I delude myself by thinking
it will make people understand the futility of hate.

Brian L., Vietnam, 1972

By the early 1970s, more than four years after taking up the pen on Juliet's behalf, Beltramini's identity as the author of hundreds of thoughtful replies was ultimately revealed in a book about the city, *Il Colore di Verona,* by journalist Arnaldo Bellini. It's impossible to know if Beltramini had agreed to this unmasking; he and Bellini were good friends. What is certain is that immediately after the book's publication, Beltramini tendered his resignation to the head of Verona's tourism office, explaining that the burden of answering the missives, which had grown from around fifty to more than three hundred annually, had become too much. When news of his decision reached the general public through several magazine and newspaper articles, it prompted an influx of letters, addressed not to Juliet but directly to Beltramini.

Dear Gino Beltramini,
I have read in our local newspaper of your position as
letter writer to the Municipality of Verona charged with
the task of answering letters to Romeo and Juliet. It
saddens me to hear that you feel the work to be a burden,
so I felt compelled to write this Eastertide to wish you

*well, and to hope that you may long continue to bring joy
to numerous people all over the world.*

*Although I knew Italy only during the unhappy
years of conflict I still recall its beauty, and above all the
dignity and friendship of your countrymen in those most
difficult days.*

Once again, I wish you well,

William S., CHESHIRE, ENGLAND

Two young women wrote this letter of appreciation:

Dear Prof. Beltramini,
*We think that you have done a great service to those who
have written to you for a word of advice or just to get
something off their chests, and we ask you to continue....
Continue! Many people need a good word, or some
advice, to get their courage back, to go on.*

PINEROLO, ITALY

Another woman paid her compliments and attempted to extract
some advice from the outgoing secretary:

Dear Prof. Beltramini,

I've just come to learn about you through my favorite magazine, La Famiglia Cristiana. *I think it is wonderful what you're doing for the many unhappy souls who write to you from all over the world. I hope you won't give up this mission of yours. There aren't many people like you! Perhaps you might ask yourself why I'm writing to you. I'll get straight to the point. I am an American girl living in a small Italian town. I, too, hold correspondence from several parts of the world. I know what listening to other people's problems means, and what it means to help them out. But now I need your help. Could you please get me in touch with a twenty-five to twenty-eight year old (the age is very important!) American man in Vietnam? I want to hear about the experiences of someone over there. I hope that you won't think I'm not serious. I am very serious. Please, if this is possible, send me word at the enclosed address.*

I'm depending on you. Thank you,

S.P.L., Asti, Italy, 1972

A friend of Beltramini's, the popular dialectical poet Gino Tomaselli known as "Café Nero," wrote from Treviso in 1972:

> *What you are doing is a thing of such lofty and moving poetry that it isn't right that you should stop. I am convinced that all of Verona would rise up so that Juliet of our dreams could live and write, since so many turn to her for a word of faith, of love, and of hope. Bravo, bravo! I had no clue about your high and noble undertaking.*

Beltramini was unmoved. His contribution to the ongoing correspondence between writers from around the globe and Shakespeare's heroine was over. Yet his final remarks to Bellini about the phenomenon still resonate.

Juliet's mail reveals an important truth. The world has changed, but only on the outside. The mechanism of modern progress has given an entirely different exterior structure to our existence than that of the past. But man has remained, in reality, with the essential elements of life. We only have different forms of expression, but the fundamental theme is always the same: love. All men, and women, who write do so spurred by disappointment. At this point it is necessary to rebuild their feelings, and trust, and to invite them to look for real love, not its surrogate: the dazzling of the senses.

After Beltramini's death in 1983, his daughter compiled a complete bibliography of his extensive writings, in which she also noted the manuscripts left unfinished. Among these was a project for a "Sentimental Guide to Verona," a twenty-three-chapter volume conceived to "explain Verona through the eyes of the Veronese people before their centuries-old traditions disappear or are changed completely." The first chapter, largely complete, summarized the city's history through the early Middle Ages. Chapter two was to be devoted to Romeo and Juliet.

Beltramini's resignation had no effect on the mail. The letters to Juliet continued, delivered in large batches to the municipal building, where they again posed a dilemma for the city. Since there was no Beltramini-like figure waiting in the wings, the Protocol Office decided that Juliet's mail should be forwarded to the Estate Teatrale Veronese, the organization responsible for the summer theater season held in Verona's first-century Roman theater.

This choice may seem arbitrary, given the many sectors within the city's convoluted bureaucracy dedicated to cultural and tourism activities. Yet there is a logical historical connection. Verona's renowned Shakespeare festival, held annually at the Roman theater since 1948, launched its opening season with a sold-out production of *Romeo and Juliet*, directed by the Veronese composer and librettist Renato Simoni.

 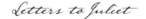

So rather than continuing to accumulate in the city offices, the letters instead piled up on the desk of the theater's artistic director, Gian Paolo Savorelli. Not quite sure what to do with them, Savorelli turned to his secretary and asked her to reply to the best of her ability. Whenever she had a few spare moments, she dashed off answers to writers from around the world (friends pitched in with translation help), signing them, "Secretary to Juliet." The city picked up the postage bill. Though exceedingly uncomfortable with interviews and press conferences, and insisting that she be anonymous, the secretary quickly grew passionate about her task and began to dedicate time far beyond her work hours. "I felt bad seeing those letters lying unopened on my desk," she says. "I did my best to give every one an answer, even if just a few lines."

This improvised handling of Juliet's mail, begun in the mid-1970s out of a sense of duty and, as Savorelli puts it, "in recognition of Shakespeare's great contribution to Verona," endured for nearly a decade. In 1984, the secretary was transferred to another city office and relinquished her role. Once again, Juliet was silenced.

CHAPTER SIX

Club di Giulietta

*W*alking into the Club di Giulietta a visitor might think that
she had stumbled into the backstage area of a small theater.
Nothing on the outside of this nondescript building in this nondescript neighborhood hints at the magical atmosphere that is revealed
when the door is opened. Mannequins outfitted in medieval costumes,
movie posters, miscellaneous tiaras, and a maquette for a pair of
bronze Romeo and Juliet doors are among the hodgepodge of objects
all casually arranged around a large round wooden table, painted
bright red, on which rest archives of letters from years past. Romeo,
the club's tomcat, is there, too, angling for a rubdown.

Beyond the table is an office area with phones, a copy machine,
and a computer for handling the copious correspondence received
via email. A few smaller rooms along one side of the space serve as
extra offices and storage for the more than 50,000 letters—all received
since 1989.

MAILBOX, CLUB DI GIULIETTA

101

Giulio Tamassia

There's more to see. A sharp turn to the right and the visitor is welcomed onto center-stage, the office of the club's founder and president, Giulio Tamassia, who presides over the goings-on from behind an expansive desk strewn with books, papers, and multiple telephones. On a nearby wall, adjacent to drawings by his grandchild, a small oil-on-canvas portrait of William Shakespeare provides the crowning touch to this exquisitely disheveled lair. But wait. That's not Shakespeare's likeness protruding from the ruffled collar but a precise rendering of Tamassia himself, in full Elizabethan dress. A dapper man, with a deep baritone and a conspiratorial glint behind thick boxy glasses, Tamassia is the undisputed keeper of the flame.

His devotion to Juliet and her legend began more than thirty years ago, in 1972, when he and several friends, united by a love for their city and a determination to keep its traditions and legends alive, founded an informal club bearing her name. Every two weeks this group of musicians, artists, journalists, and other interested denizens met in their attic headquarters. Membership for women was strictly forbidden. As Tamassia explains, their presence would have impeded one of the principal topics of conversation: women. On the rare occasion that wives and companions were welcomed, they were hosted with great chivalry.

Dinner was at eight sharp (latecomers were fined!), cooked by the members in the club's kitchen and accompanied by good wine and conversation that leaned toward politics and problems related to the city's cultural life.

The club's activities were not limited to meals and lengthy debates. Many notable poets and musicians passed through this salon over the years for extemporaneous readings in Veronese dialect and performances, and members of the group organized informal events in theaters around town. When a problem irked them, the more literarily inclined dashed off a letter to city officials expressing their opinions.

The city took note of their zeal. When faced in the late 1980s with Juliet's mail (the "secret" secretary had left her post a few years earlier) the cultural commissioner, Alfredo Meocci, familiar with Tamassia's can-do manner, called him to see if he knew of someone who could reply to the mountain of letters sitting unopened in his office. Tamassia gamely offered his services. "If no one answered her mail," he says with characteristic pragmatism, "the phenomenon would have stopped."

With zero support from the city (the fiscal year had already begun and there was no money budgeted for stamps), Tamassia found a young Mexican student who had come to Verona to learn Italian and was fluent in French and English as well as her native Spanish. Coached by Tamassia, who also drafted the occasional reply, she gradually eliminated the backlog of mail and took on the new arrivals. Her impressive language skills allowed her to handle the bulk of the correspondence on her own, but when necessary she and Tamas-sia turned to neighborhood acquaintances for translation help. The owner of a Chinese restaurant and a Turkish NATO official were particularly obliging. Their generous assistance notwithstanding, the workload was becoming too much for a single secretary determined to compose a handwritten reply to each letter on Juliet's personal sta-tionery. So two additional young women, each with bilingual skills and unrelated full-time occupations, joined the effort in their spare time. An office was required. With typical alacrity, Tamassia located one within a centrally located music school.

The inauguration of this first official seat, used exclusively for letter-writing activities, marked the rebirth of the Club di Giulietta. (The meetings of the earlier incarnation were increasingly sporadic, due to natural attrition and members' commitments elsewhere.) And it coincided with Tamassia's retirement from his job as general man-ager of one of Verona's main industrial bakeries, allowing him to dedicate his undivided attention to Juliet and her future.

The letters continued to arrive, increasing in number and lan-guages, and captivating the attention of the international press. Front-page stories about Tamassia and his "Juliets" appeared in the early 1990s in the *Wall Street Journal*, the *Washington Post*, and *Le Figaro*, among other publications, unleashing a torrent of correspondence; to this day, wherever articles on the Club di Giulietta appear, letters from that area increase dramatically for a time.

More secretaries were needed and, naturally, Tamassia found them. First he convinced his youngest daughter to answer some of the German and English letters. Her part-time work in an import-export company left her a few free hours during the week, hours that she could devote to Juliet! Her role quickly grew, and she soon transferred her energies, full-time, to the club. Tamassia then recruited the daughter of a friend who was interested in the letters and eager to use her high school English. Before long, a full-time assistant joined the group. An extrovert with a way with numbers, she did double duty as bookkeeper and press liaison. And, of course, she answered the mail, specializing in letters from younger writers.

At the club's onset, the Juliets had devised a meticulous registration and archiving system to ensure that every letter was logged in, answered, and preserved. (With the exception of a few early examples, copies of the replies were never kept.) More letters meant more paper, and more secretaries to handle it. The club was outgrowing its home.

This was all good news to Tamassia. The space crunch was proof that the Juliet correspondence deserved even more recognition. In 1993, with support from the city, which by now was paying the club's postage bill, he created the Cara Giulietta prize, an annual award for the best letter, selected from among the thousands received by the club each year.

The winner—or, sometimes, winners—is contacted by the club and invited to spend an all-expenses-paid weekend in Verona, where the award ceremony is held on Valentine's Day, at Juliet's house. The late actress Giulietta Masina was the prize's first "godmother," followed in 1994 by the Italian ballerina Carla Fracci. Leonard Whiting,

Juliet's Birthday

NURSE: *Faith, I can tell her age unto an hour.*
LADY CAPULET: *She's not fourteen.*
NURSE: *I'll lay fourteen of my teeth—*
    And yet, to my teen be it spoken, I have but four—
    She's not fourteen. How long is it now
    To Lammas-tide?
LADY CAPULET: *A fortnight and odd days.*
NURSE: *Even or odd, of all days in the year,*
    Come Lammas Eve at night shall she be fourteen.

✸

Shakespeare tells us that Juliet was born on July 31, one day before Lammas-tide, an early English church harvest festival celebrated on August 1. Some scholars think that he chose July for her birthday simply because his protagonist's name was Juliet.

For Giulio Tamassia, who was planning to stage a medieval festival in Verona on the occasion of the heroine's birthday, this date did not sit well at all. Northern Italy is hot and humid in midsummer, and city dwellers escape to the seaside and nearby mountains in droves. Virtually no one would be in town. He sought the advice of Giuseppe Franco Viviani, a director of the Verona city libraries at the time, who assembled several historians, as well as an astronomer, to study the problem.

After consulting the original da Porto text ("she has already passed her eighteenth year on Saint Euphemia's Day last"), and taking into account the calendar reform decreed by Pope Gregory XIII in 1582, the group concluded that Juliet was born September 16, the day that Saint Euphemia is venerated in Verona, in the year 1284. Shakespeare's Juliet is inexplicably four years younger, but never mind. Mid-September is lovely in Verona and, as far as Tamassia was concerned, an ideal time for the festival.

O ROMEO, ROMEO, WHEREFORE ART THOU ROMEO?
(GOUACHE ON PAPER), WILLIAM HATHERELL, C. 1912

Franco Zeffirelli's Romeo, was the club's special guest at the 2004 ceremony.

The success of this prize motivated Tamassia to organize other initiatives around the myth of the Shakespearean lovers. In September 1993, he put together an annual medieval festival that takes place in the Piazza dei Signori and features costumed dancers, theatrical performers, arts and crafts, and an open-air painting marathon to coincide with Juliet's birthday. One hundred artists, from Verona and beyond, are invited to set up their easels in the piazza and, in just one day, complete a painting dedicated to the theme of Romeo and Juliet or, failing that, love in general.

The resulting higher profile of the Club di Giulietta prompted some municipal officials to worry that Juliet—whom they felt belonged to the city—was slipping from their grasp. So, in the mid-1990s, Tamassia was contacted and asked to bring Juliet's mail to the city's cultural affairs office. Unhappy, but loath to argue with an order from on high, Tamassia and the secretaries glumly delivered several bags of unopened mail to the municipal building.

With the letters now in the city's possession, the staff of the cultural affairs office was asked if any of them might be interested in taking a stab at answering the correspondence. Three women and a man with a good knowledge of English offered to try, and were given the letters to read and respond to on top of their usual jobs.

When interviewed some years later and asked if they had been given any guidelines for answering the mail, one of the city secretaries said that they were instructed to refer to Shakespeare's text and, using lines from the play, to reply exclusively in English. When pressed she confessed that, though she had taken on the task with great enthusiasm, this constraint made it extremely difficult to compose satisfactory answers to the wide range of letters that crossed her desk.

The endeavor proved frustrating for everyone involved, and the cultural commissioner at the time soon understood that although Juliet is indeed Veronese, and her story contributes greatly to the city's allure and mystique, not just anyone could handle her mail. After making amends with Tamassia—who declares he holds no grudges—the official gave the mail back to the club and its secretaries—who had been waiting patiently—and became one of the operation's greatest champions.

Now that the mail was back where it belonged, the club could no longer delay moving into larger offices. The question was where. The impossibly high rents and parking problems in the city center impelled Tamassia to move the whole operation to the groundfloor apartment of a building he owned just a short drive from downtown. With space no longer an issue, more secretaries gradually joined the effort to keep up with the mail. There are currently nine, and their diverse backgrounds and collective command of English, German, Spanish, French, Japanese, and a smattering of other languages in addition to Italian enable them to reply to every letter and email. When the occasional indecipherable letter arrives, the secretaries mine their extensive network of friends and colleagues to decode and respond, often in English, the established common language.

Not too long ago, a letter arrived in braille. A translator was quickly found and a reply promptly mailed.

So what drew them to this task? Apart from the initial few who knew Tamassia personally, the others entered the fold by chance or, in a few cases, by design. One secretary, a professional dancer, met the club crew while performing at one of Verona's annual medieval festivals. Hearing the letters discussed at a post-performance dinner, she was intrigued and asked to learn more. She has been replying since 1996. Another, who teaches at a middle school, encountered the club while undertaking an academic study of the letters and was invited to try her hand at a few replies. Instantly hooked, she has been a secretary for eight years. Tamassia's full-time assistant, brought on in 2002 to help with the organization's multiple endeavors, including its magazine, *Cara Giulietta*, replies to the ever-increasing onslaught of emails, answering in English and Spanish, and maintains the club's Web site, which she helped create. She also keeps the mercurial Tamassia on schedule.

Though in most cases, their day jobs bear no relationship to their secretarial work, when they pick up the pen in Juliet's name they are

JULIET'S SECRETARIES

remarkably in sync. They undergo no official instruction or scrutiny (Tamassia has weeded out only a few unsuitable secretaries over the years), and there is a palpable feeling of teamwork in the office. They routinely share letters and consult one another about their responses. The rare, particularly troubling letter is referred to the club's sixteen-year veteran, who has a keen interest in psychology. All agree that empathy and common sense are the universal guidelines.

"Juliet is the eternal symbol of love and each person imagines her according to his or her own desires," explains one of the most experienced secretaries. "Most of the people who write to her are looking for a way to unburden themselves, to share their problems with someone who will listen, unconditionally, as if she were a friend, or confidante.

"The thousands of letters we receive each year are proof that personal problems are universal. Whether the letters arrive from France, Japan, or Brazil, allowing for small cultural variants, the prevailing themes are unrequited love, falling for a person who is already married or otherwise involved, problems stemming from loneliness, and, to a lesser degree, differences of religion, race, and culture."

The fact that the secretaries don't receive more letters that comment on pressing social or political issues doesn't strike her as strange. "It's not a matter of selfishness or a sad sign of the times," she says. "It is more that you may be a politician, a housewife, an accountant, a war correspondent . . . whatever. But if you take your pen to write Juliet a letter you *want* to put aside the outside world to concentrate on the most intimate aspects of your life.

"Another way of seeing it is that only dreamers write to Juliet. So it is only natural for them to be escapist. Occasionally they might mention a dreadful social or political situation as a way of explaining their need to talk to someone living in another dimension.

"Our job is to give those who write a word of consolation and a ray of hope and, at times, more concrete suggestions. There is always something positive to latch on to, and we try to help even the most desperate writers see where to find it."

Adolescents often seek practical advice, like how to get a boy or girl to notice them, or how to ask for a date. The few who comment on Juliet's suicide tend to scold her and tell her that she was foolish to take her life for Romeo. Yet, at the same time, they admire the courage and decisiveness she demonstrated in standing up to her family.

Not everyone writes with a serious problem. Many letters are effusive testimonials to happiness. Others seek a blessing, some sort of spiritual protection, for their love. They write to Juliet as if she were a saint, recalling some of the earliest notes left at her tomb site.

Occasional writers, almost all male—and often around Valentine's Day—contact Juliet and request that she intervene on their behalf, asking her to compose a letter to a wife, girlfriend, or lover. Some confess that though they deeply love the person in question, and desire to express these feelings in words, they are incapable of doing so. Juliet, of course, always obliges, and she has received many grateful notes from these tongue-tied Romeos confirming the success of her epistolary mission.

Dear Juliet,

Please send a letter to Melissa H. for me. Here is her address. It should read:

> *"My dear Melissa,*
>
> *Like my Romeo, your Justin has declared his love and devotion for you. May your hearts be one as are mine and Romeo's.*
>
> *With love, Juliet*
> *Verona, Italy"*

Of course I would be glad to forward a donation to your organization to help with your various postage costs, etc. Please let me know if this can be done as it would mean so much to my dearest Melissa.

Sincerely,

Justin R., Milwaukee, Wisconsin

Dear Justin,

I will certainly do what you ask me. There is no need to
send anything! I really hope that your love will be as deep
as ours . . . but also much luckier!

Lots of love to you both,

Juliet

Ten days later:

Dear Juliet,

Thank you, thank you! My dear Milli received the letter
and it made her week so nice and happy. I appreciate
your kindness and will try to pass it on by being extra
kind to someone today.

Thanks again,

Justin

Nearly all of the Juliets working today have been with the club for several years, and each says, without exception, that she would sorely miss the task were she to stop replying. This dedication has freed Tamassia to look beyond the letters, and in 1996 he created the Scrivere per Amore prize, awarded annually to a novel published in Italy that addresses the theme of love, interpreted as broadly as possible. The jury is made up of a changing roster of prominent writers, professors, and cultural figures.

Given the inventive mix of festivals, literary competitions, and other events orchestrated by Tamassia and his assistants, it is not surprising that the Club di Giulietta has become a de facto branch of the cultural affairs office, and Tamassia its emissary. Visiting journalists inevitably find their way here, as do visual artists, musicians, and other performers who pass through the city. All are welcomed. Questions are answered. Espresso is served. Yet at the end of the day no single activity takes higher priority than the mail addressed to Juliet.

From Russia with Love

Far from Verona lives a diminutive blond named Olga, who feels a powerful connection to Juliet. Since reading the play and seeing the Zeffirelli film as an adolescent, the Moscow resident has identified with Shakespeare's heroine and filled numerous albums with press clippings, photographs, and other memorabilia related to the story. Fortunately, her own Romeo, husband Vladimir, shares her passion; together they have created an elaborate Web site that includes photographs from their various trips to Verona to visit the places associated with the myth. One shot shows them on Juliet's balcony, in full Renaissance dress. Another captures a pensive Olga at the tomb.

Their involvement with the tale goes beyond veneration to the practical. Since 1997 they have anchored the Moscow branch of the Club di Giulietta, fielding letters in Russian that are forwarded to them from the Verona office. "Olga's a great help to us," comments a Verona-based secretary. "She shares our passion and commitment. And, after all, none of us knows Russian!"

Dear Juliet,

Last March I wrote you a letter (I am attaching a photocopy) to which you kindly replied. You also wrote a letter to my wife, as I had asked you to. And the miracle happened. Love triumphed, and my wife has returned. We are living together again, with our children. We are all very happy. For this we owe you a great deal. I am certain you have magical power, the power to give great love.

    I thank you profoundly,

                            Marc L., CANNES, FRANCE

Dear Juliet,

I know this girl who sometimes kind of likes me and sometimes doesn't, and I want to know what star-crossed lovers are. Does this have to do with birthdays? Mine is August 11, 1979, and hers is April 28, 1981, if that helps. Sometimes I offer to carry her books home from school, but she just thinks I'm kidding, and her friend who walks home with her hits me. I used to joke around with her and she'd kick me, but now she's stopped kicking me. Every time my friends think I say something that makes them think I like her, they yell out, "You like

Emily!" But they don't know I LOVE her. So, how do I get her to go out with me?

Sincerely,

Andrew J., RIVERTON, UTAH, 1993

❧

I often think of Juliet: she was sweet and innocent like an angel, but she knew love, tears, and pain at an early age. I am only a few years older than she, but I don't yet have a boyfriend. If only I could be there, on that balcony, be there and dream for a moment! But only the dreams of the night can realize my desires.

Feruzah N., UZBEKISTAN

❧

Dear Juliet,
Why did you not go with Romeo to Mantua? You could have told your parents the truth when he was banished and then left with him. But instead, you and Friar Laurence devised a scheme that had little chance of working. If you were not so impetuous, perhaps you and Romeo would be alive and well. But you were truly in love with Romeo; you had to be, otherwise you wouldn't

have trusted the friar at all. Do you blame your deaths on the adults? After all, it was an adult's plan that killed you and Romeo. Despite your less than wise decisions, I admire you, Juliet. You are very brave and have the courage of an army. You followed your true love even though he was the enemy of your beloved family. I believe that in each one of us there is a little bit of you. You will be remembered as one of the fairest ladies of Italy. I really enjoyed reading your story. Please write me back and tell me what you think.

Sincerely,

Caroline R., Greensborough,
North Carolina, 1994

Dear Juliet,
I have liked a boy named Julian for a long time now. We're both in the ninth grade and take piano lessons from the same teacher. I like how nice he is to all the people around him. I only wish he were about four inches taller because that would put us at the same height. I found out today that he has a date to the winter dance. I'm afraid that if I show any signs of liking him more than as a friend he won't talk to me. Juliet, I don't mean to be rude, but I think you married Romeo a little too hastily. I think

I should wait until I figure out how Julian feels about me, especially if he is dating another girl. Maybe by that time he'll be taller too! What do you think? In my opinion, parting with Julian is such sweet sorrow.

    Sincerely,

Amy G., Iowa City, Iowa

✿

Hello! Giulietta!

Do you remember me? I wrote to you some time ago. Thank you very much for your response. I was very happy. A postman came when I was watching TV. He said: "Good day! I can't understand what's written here. It's in English." I realized that it was a letter from you. The next day I told my schoolmates about it. They didn't believe it at first, but I showed them the letter and after that they did. I'm very grateful to you for your wishes to me, despite my being a Chechen, because some people don't like us. I think you are a very kind girl. I'd like to be a little like you. If only I could have my photo taken with you and Leonardo DiCaprio! I'd be the happiest girl in the world. I'm sending you my photo, Giulietta. Please, send me a letter again.

    Your admirer,

Elina Z., Grozny, Chechnya, 2003

Dear Juliet,

I read about your Club in a magazine, and thought I saw a firefly in the darkness. I just want to find all the information about a Chinese man, Yun Di Li, who won the Chopin piano contest. I find I have fallen in love with him for his music. Because I am not attractive, I must ask others to help. Can you tell me his email? How can I have access to him? I know he is a favorite pianist and has his own world. I only want to help him covertly. I hope I could comfort him, and ease his pain when he is depressed. I hope you can help me, and look forward to your answer.

    Thanks,

                    Cari B., Beijing, China, 2003

Dear Juliet,

I was wondering if I could get some advice on a problem I have. You see, I really like a girl but my parents won't let me date her for religious reasons. Should I defy them and secretly date her, or should I listen to my parents? I await your reply eagerly.

    From,

                    Joseph L., Mesa, Arizona, 2003

Dear Juliet,

*I'm coming to you with something that has been
bothering me for a while. My algebra grade is dropping
dramatically. I got my midterm back today and I have a
65 in that class. I've tried everything but still can't make
an A or even a high B.*

Please help!

Angela G., CALHOUN, GEORGIA, 1995

Hello Juliet,

*My name is Viktar and I live in the beautiful city of
Mozyr. I want to tell my love story, of a love that I
had then lost and still can't understand why. During a
military leave, I met a girl. It was a magic night. She
was as beautiful as an angel on earth, with marvelous
eyes, and a special way of talking. . . . I had never met a
woman like her. With the passage of days and weeks our
feelings grew; when I returned to service we wrote letters
and poems to each other. My friends didn't recognize
me, so much was I changed. That was the most beautiful
time of my life.*

MOZYR, BELARUS

Dear Juliet,

I need some advice on girls. Christmas is coming up and I don't know what to get my friend. She's really nice and I like her a lot. I was thinking of getting her a bracelet, but what kind? I can't afford diamonds, so I know that's out. I'm thinking of asking her out when I give it to her. Do girls like poems and candy? I know they like candles and lots of jewelry. Should I get her a bracelet or a necklace? What kind of necklace?

Please write back!

Sincerely,

Gene O., DENVER, COLORADO

***

Dear Juliet,

A few months ago I was at camp in Nevada. While I was there I met many people I grew close to. Among them was my friend Peter. Two years ago he found out he was HIV positive. It is believed he contracted the virus from a contaminated needle at a health clinic when he was younger. Our only contact now is through letters and phone calls. His parents don't encourage much correspondence and he is not allowed to visit any of his friends from camp. People avoid him because they are scared of the virus. I can understand their fear but it is

unjustified. He is so alone and no one will reach out
to him.

I can't accept the fact that he is dying. It makes me
angry and there is nothing I can do about it. I want to be
able to tell him everything is going to be fine. But I know
that it isn't and don't know what to say. Can you tell me
what I should say to help him?

Yours truly,

Hilary B., STATEN ISLAND, NEW YORK, 1995

Dear Juliet,
My friend is having a bad life. She says she wants to kill
herself. I am very afraid for her. Sometimes it scares me
so much. I cry for her, and I usually don't cry. I would
like to know what I can do for her before it's too late.
Please help.

Sincerely,

Mark S., BELLEVIEW, WASHINGTON, 1991

Dear Juliet,

Two years ago my parents separated. We were happy all together. Now, my father lives with another woman and my mother with another man. This situation makes me very unhappy, and I wish everything could be like before. I do everything I can to make this happen, but they never stop arguing. I've had enough!

Help me!

Nicole B., JOINVILLE-LE-PONT, FRANCE, 1998

Dear Juliet,

You are the only person I can ask. How do you French kiss and what does it mean to make out? I read an article about you in the paper and if we write to you and I get a letter back we get extra credit. And I need a lot of extra credit.

Thank you,

Sandra J., CONSTANTIA, NEW YORK, 1993

Dear Juliet,
I have been married for three years and I am in love
with my husband. I would like it if he would surprise me
sometimes, if he would buy me a present now and again,
but he says he is a confirmed non-romantic. I want to
believe in the fable, in eternal love. I believe that it is the
little things of little importance that make life on this
earth beautiful. It is our sun, and the little golden rays
that shine through the clouds of the everyday routine that
remind us how beautiful life really is, in defiance of its
banal reality. Perhaps, Juliet, you could write to him and
tell him something about romance.

Habiba Z., AL KHAWR, QATAR

✥

Dear Romeo, Dear Juliet,
Two of our dearest friends were just married, at age fifty,
after many years of reflection. She lived on the first floor
of our condominium, he on the second. After meeting
many times on the stairs, they got married. It was a
beautiful wedding, because there was so much love, and
because they wanted to be joined forever, like Romeo and
Juliet. What we want to ask of you, Romeo and Juliet,
lovers for eternity, is that you write them a short good-
luck letter. We thank you warmly, and again say "bravo"

and thanks to all of the volunteers who keep the legend of the celebrated lovers alive.

Your friends,

Roger and Claire K., MONTMORILLON, FRANCE, 1998

Dear Juliet,

I've been married to my wife, Shannon, for thirty years. I have never made love to another woman, let alone kissed another. Despite our advancing years we are still like young lovers. We steal kisses and passionately embrace when no one is around. Well, even when others are around!

Although we are of modest means I derive the greatest pleasure in giving her small gifts, spending time with her at a local café, or walking together along the shore near our home. But now that we are getting older I am sad that I have been unable to give her more in life or take her to exotic or far-flung places. I want the whole world to know how much I love her, and who better to help me do that than you, dear Juliet! I would like it if you were to write to her telling her of my devotion so she can have a keepsake to pass on to our daughter.

Yours sincerely,

Benjamin K., EAST FREMANTLE, AUSTRALIA, 1991

Juliet,

At the moment, I am listening to the music from
Romeo + Juliet, with Leonardo DiCaprio and Claire
Danes.

    I decided to write to you because I am desperately
alone, and I no longer believe in a "great love." I am
going to be twenty-eight next April but I haven't found
my "Romeo."

Bella Y., Nice, France, 2001

❧

Dear Juliet,

I have arrived at a time in my life when I am faced
with a major dilemma. I have been with a young man
for nearly two years and I am very much in love with
him and I know he loves me too. The problem is that I
was raised in a strict Catholic family. My parents didn't
permit me to date until I was eighteen and, in their
definition, mature. The young man that I am seeing
is neither Catholic nor Italian, like my family. He is
Jewish. My parents are not prejudiced. However, I know
that they do not want to relinquish the dreams they
have of me marrying a nice Italian Catholic boy. I have
discussed with him the many conflicts that might arise
when he is introduced to my family as my fiancé, but he

says that he refuses to stop seeing me. He is willing to convert to Catholicism to please my parents, but I don't think it's fair to ask him to leave behind everything he's been raised to believe in. I know that if I had decided to convert to Judaism my parents would be very upset with me. I love him more than I ever imagined possible, but I do love my religion more. What should I do?

Marilyn F., Iowa City, Iowa, 1995

✢

Dear Giulietta,
I'm just a basic, no-frills Aussie boy in my mid-thirties still looking for the one and only. I heard about your address, and thought you, being the romantic one, could give me a hand. I live in the N.S.W. country town of Griffith, working on farms growing trees, ornamental flowers, and roses. The roses are my favorite. It is such a pleasure to see the flowers burst after all the time and work. Anyway, I'd love to babble on. All the best for Christmas and New Year's.

Love always,

Andrew G., Griffith, Australia, 2003
P.S. Please send rain.

Cara Signora,
I appeal to you for a favor. I have daughter, twenty-seven,
who has never been married but is looking for a fiancé.
Is it possible for you to look for a fiancé for her? Is it
possible for her to be married in Verona? How much
does a modest wedding there cost? We are Orthodox! Is
this a problem? Is there a waiting list for this? Here is
my address. I will be very happy to receive your reply.

Svetlana C., Kiev, Ukraine, 2003

❧

What a wonderful thing you do! I am a priest. We both
work in the Service of Love, each of us in our own way.
God bless your good hearts!

Father Guilbert M., Fatima, Portugal, 2003

❧

Dear Juliet,
I will be so glad in my heart to get your reply. Really!
You know, I graduated from university last year and
work in a travel bureau of Guang Dong province. I miss
my boyfriend very much; we haven't seen each other
for over a year. The reason is that he's from Taiwan
and I'm from Mainland China. If you understand the

relationship between Taiwan and Mainland China you will know this is not strange.

After the SARS situation here everyone cherishes life more, including me. But at the same time I cherish my love, as it's not easy to find someone who loves you, and he really is an excellent man, believe me. There are too many words I want to tell you but I need time, right? I wish you good luck in your work and life! Give my love to your family and friends! I'm looking forward to getting your sincere letter!

Your friend,

Lili C., GUANGZHOU, CHINA, 2003

Dear Juliet,
I am heartbroken. I am only fourteen years old and a girl and I live in India. I am in love with a GIRL, and in India lesbians are never heard of. We are, or should I say, we were, in love. We were just great until my mom found out that her family is not well off and has a shady background and is fighting some court case. She told me to break off all ties with Divya (that's my love's name). Mom does not know of our love. Neither do her parents. I told Divya that we had to hide our friendship along with our love and she took it as an insult. Divya is very

*complex. I love her, love her, and I cannot forget her. I'm
in a mess. Please, only you can understand my problem.*

Aaina G., DELHI, INDIA, 2003

*Dear Members of the Club "Romeo and Juliet"!
My husband and I met each other many years ago,
thanks to Shakespeare—that is, thanks to a book of
Romeo and Juliet that I was reading sitting on a bench in
the park. In 2002 we celebrated the golden anniversary
of our marriage. We often reread the tragedy of Romeo
and Juliet ourselves. We read it to our children when they
were young, and advise our grandchildren to read it. We
think this tragedy is especially important for the young
generation now, when the best principles of love and
pure morals are trampled, when one feels fear for young
peoples' future. We'd like to thank you for your work and
promotion of Love.*

Peter and Esther N., SAMARA, RUSSIA, 2002

CHAPTER SEVEN

A Twenty-First-Century View

*And even at this day, beneath Italian skies, many a simple
girl would feel as Juliet, and many a homely gallant would
rival the extravagance of Romeo.*

SIR EDWARD BULWER-LYTTON, 1840

Locals may grumble that many tourists take a single-minded
approach to their city, but then they're accustomed to living
in the midst of a legend. "Yes, yes," they say, *"Romeo and Juliet* is
indeed a tragically beautiful story, no doubt about it. But what about
the Arena, a dazzling structure built during the first century A.D.?

"Or Castelvecchio, the magnificent 'Old Castle,' now a notewor-
thy art museum, constructed in the mid-fourteenth century at the

THE ARENA

behest of Cangrande II della Scala? Or the medieval basilica of San Zeno, whose portals are decorated with bronze reliefs depicting scenes from the Old and New Testaments and the life of Verona's patron saint?"

That these historically certifiable monuments, among many others, get short shrift is undeniable. Yet also undeniable is the appeal of the myth and of Verona itself. One of northern Italy's most enchanting cities, it is situated at the foot of the Monti Lessini, bisected by the Adige River and surrounded by stretches of walls and fortifications built over two thousand years. Steeped in the past yet resoundingly modern, the city effortlessly lends itself to fantasy.

There's nothing fossilized about the place. Somehow the juxtaposition of the ancient sites with the rushing pedestrians, cell phones plastered to their ears, and the cars and motorcyclists rocketing through the narrow streets at hair-raising speeds adds an element of possibility to the tale.

If all of these people can live here, immersed in such beauty and history, why not Juliet? Gaze down the Corso Cavour, the Roman Via Postumia, toward the double gateway at the head of Corso Portoni Borsari, and it's not at all difficult to imagine that, yes, this is where Romeo and Tybalt had their ill-fated encounter. A bronze relief on the facade of Corso Cavour, 2, describes their duel.

Let's begin where Juliet supposedly began. Smack in the center of town, at Via Cappello, 23, her house is the star attraction. The approach from the east, along Via Leone, encompasses a crazy quilt of epochs. Just past the monumental Porta Leoni on the right and the excavated remnants of the city walls dating to the Roman period are up-to-the-minute clothing and electronics stores, cafés, and gift shops. In the midst of all this commerce, sandwiched between an Armani Jeans store and a souvenir shop, is the Casa di Giulietta. There is no grand entrance, no metaphorical drum roll to signal that you're somewhere special—unless you're impressed by the ubiquitous guitar-playing gypsies, who herald your, and everyone else's, arrival.

Unlike the plastered facades of its neighbors, the worn brickwork on Juliet's house is visible, evoking an earlier era. If you look closely, a marble tablet mounted high on the worn surface hints at what is within.

These were the houses
of the Capulets
From whence Juliet sprang
For whom
So many gentle hearts have wept
and poets have sung

The scene is set. The deeply vaulted entryway, flanked by two massive iron gates, is covered in layers of colorful graffiti and blanketed by small notes stuck on every available surface. Most are simple declarations of love ("Renaldo and Annabelle forever"). Others are "I was here" messages or greetings to Juliet and Verona from various

Letters to Juliet

parts of the world. They appear to be unanimously upbeat. A few steps before the entrance to the courtyard are several primitive phone stations that narrate, in five languages, a slide show explaining the myth and the history of the house. When first installed in the 1950s, they were referred to in the city's press as "jukeboxes."

Just above the entryway, carved into the courtyard vault's keystone, is a small stone cap, which believers claim to be the Capulet family crest. The courtyard itself is surprisingly intimate and charming. Enhancing the site's fairytale-like quality are long skeins of ivy

that drape the walls and mingle with the omnipresent graffiti and notes. To the right is Juliet's house and, of course, the balcony—strategically placed and, at least from the ground, utterly convincing.

At the far end of the courtyard, under a fig tree, stands the iconic statue of Juliet. She's just about life-size, and her right breast has been rubbed to a high sheen by the hundreds of thousands of visitors who, sometimes timidly, sometimes brazenly, caress her for good luck.

Letters to Juliet

A Twenty-First-Century View 141

Letters to Juliet

All this attention doesn't seem to disturb her regal composure. To the statue's right is a gift shop selling mass-produced story-related merchandise, the only jarring element in the courtyard.

On an early morning visit in late November, the yard is filled with an international crowd of visitors. A small Christmas tree stands in the center; it too is festooned with messages. Kids are climbing everywhere, sticking up notes, posing with Juliet. Two people step onto the balcony and look out. The mood here is positively boisterous. Friends are documenting one another, the cell phone camera the instrument of choice. Though some messages apparently require extra security, or symbolism, and are secured with tiny padlocks to the house's window gratings, most are stuck to the walls with chewing gum.

Most tourists confine their visits to the courtyard. There's no admission fee and it provides an ideal view of the all-important balcony. But don't leave without venturing inside the house, where another, slightly more subdued gift shop snares visitors the moment they enter the front door. There are some good books and postcards but they can wait. Pay the modest fee, and the attendant will direct you up the wooden staircase to the main room, presumably the scene of the Capulets' masked ball.

Remembered images from the various films don't mesh with what's actually here. There's nothing sumptuous about the room. The wide-planked wooden floor, plastered walls, and painted ceiling are remarkably simple yet effective. The austere high-backed wooden chairs scattered about, the antique chest of drawers pushed up against

Update:
The Gum Conundrum

A few years ago an enterprising tourist discovered that used chewing gum was the perfect adherent, starting a gum-gluing craze that threatened to wreak havoc on the ancient bricks of Juliet's house. In 2005, the city removed the gum, cordoning off sections of the yard bit by bit. A debate raged as to how to discourage further gum gluing once the cleaning was completed. Some people favored covering the walls with Plexiglas, a barrier that would protect the bricks but certainly disrupt the sense of magic. Others recommended a digital solution in which love notes could be "delivered" to Juliet via cell phone text message or email and immediately posted at computer stations within the house.

For now, the walls of the vaulted courtyard entrance have been covered with white plasterboard. Visitors are encouraged to express themselves on this surface—and this surface only—which is periodically scraped down and repainted. The presence of a guard seems, so far, to be inhibiting infractions.

one wall, and the emblematic paintings evoke the atmosphere of a theater set anticipating the arrival of the performers. A guest book positioned at one end of the room records visitors' comments. A quick sampling reveals messages in Korean, Russian, Italian, Spanish, French, English, and Norwegian. "I just had to visit after thirty years," from Australia. "Waiting for true, pure love," from Brazil. "Happy birthday, Martin my brother," from Prague. "I love you, my wife," from Punjab, India. "Romeo, where are you my love?" from England. Some sign their notes with a heart: "Hi, Grandpa, I love you so much! ♥"

A low wall with rounded vaults and pairs of slender columns divides the main part of the space from a smaller area with a stone floor. The balcony is here, immediately to the left. It's surprisingly shallow; there's barely enough room to turn around. Antonio Avena, the mastermind behind this and many other "medievalized" sites in the city, had a keen theatrical intelligence. He knew that the perspective from below conveyed the appropriate scale, and that the trompe l'oeil effect would kick in when visitors experienced the drama of actually standing on Juliet's balcony.

The second floor, reached via a graceful if stylistically incongruous

Being Juliet

The first time Juliet appeared onstage, she was a he—most likely a young performer named Robert Goffe. It was the Elizabethan era, and though theater was a popular pastime the theaters were notoriously filthy and, in the eyes of the Puritans and the Church of England, actors were considered morally dubious at best. Women were not allowed onstage. So men and boys played all roles, no matter the gender in the playscript.

This practice continued until 1642, when the Puritan Parliament finally brought theatrical life in England to an abrupt halt. The theaters remained dark until King Charles II took the throne in 1660, paving the way for the Restoration. Now women, rather than boys, were cast in the female roles. Mary Saunderson, the first verifiable Juliet, appeared in a 1662 production. (The director, Sir William Davenant, may have been Shakespeare's illegitimate son.) Saunderson's performance, along with the entire production, was famously panned by the diarist Samuel Pepys: ". . . and thence to the Opera, and there saw 'Romeo and Juliet,' the first time it was ever acted; but it is a play of itself the worst that ever I heard in my life, and the worst acted that ever I saw these people do."

This inauspicious debut aside, Juliet has gone on to great theatrical heights through the nuanced interpretations of, among others, Eleonora Duse, Katherine Cornell, Edda Albertini, Dames Peggy Ashcroft and Judi Dench, and Francesca Annis.

She's also been realized through song. In 1830 the soprano Giulia Grisi brought Vincenzo Bellini's Juliet to operatic life. Thirty-seven years later Marie Miolan-Carvalho originated the role in Charles-François Gounod's opera *Roméo et Juliette*, a triumphant premiere that prompted a hundred-night extension.

Juliet began her life on-screen in a number of silent films, including a 1916 release starring a haunted-looking Theda Bara. We first heard Juliet speak in George Cukor's 1936 blockbuster. Norma Shearer, then a postadolescent thirty-four, couldn't help but give Juliet wisdom beyond her years. More film Juliets followed. In 1961, Natalie Wood played her as a love-struck urban teenager named Maria in the movie version of *West Side Story*. The young heroine regained her innocence with Olivia Hussey's portrayal in Zeffirelli's 1968 *Romeo and Juliet*. Just fifteen when the movie was shot, Hussey seems appropriately clueless and resolute. Nearly thirty years later, Claire Danes's Juliet projects an intriguing mix of modernity and Elizabethan propriety in the angst-ridden, visually arresting rendition by Baz Luhrmann.

Juliet doesn't necessarily need words to communicate. The ballerinas Tamara Karsavina, Alicia Markova, Margot Fonteyn, Carla Fracci—and, more recently, Alessandra Ferri, Alina Cojocaru, and Nina Ananiashvili—perfectly understood how to use their dancing to telegraph her naiveté and turbulence.

iron-and-wood staircase by the twentieth-century Italian architect Carlo Scarpa, maintains the simplicity of the level below. Wooden floors. A trussed ceiling. Logs placed in the fireplace, waiting to be ignited. On the wall above the mantel: a copy of the family crest, carved in stone. Several detached frescoes by Bernardino India, and others, attributed to Paolo Caliari, known as "Il Veronese," ornament the walls. It's easy to imagine Juliet mooning about in here, distracted by thoughts of Romeo.

A short walk through a glass-enclosed passageway that juts out over the courtyard leads to a small room, where two headless mannequins in climate-controlled vitrines display a set of Romeo and Juliet costumes from the Zeffirelli movie. Next to these is The Bed, on loan from a bed-manufacturing company that bought it at auction. Unlike the rest of the house, the inanimate figures and the surprisingly small bed leave little to the imagination. To the right of the Juliet figure is one of several modern bookstands distributed throughout the house. Each holds a carved wooden book open to a still from the Cukor film; on the facing page is a relevant quote from Shakespeare's play, in both Italian and English.

On to the third, penultimate floor, looking out over Via Cappello. These rooms, decorated with the stunning filigreed and geometric patterns borrowed from the della Scala era, hold more frescoes. One, a scene of the Trinity and Saints, now installed close to the ceiling, was moved here from its original spot on the outside of the building. One of the rooms is dominated by a Rube Goldbergian interactive video installation where visitors can learn about the legend

and send email messages directly to Juliet, via the Club di Giulietta. We fire off one on the spot, asking her how she feels about the Internet. The red metal mailbox that used to be in the courtyard is here as well, stuck behind this contraption. A handful of letters has been shoved through its slot.

Lucky for us, we bump into one of the club's secretaries, here to collect the day's mail. We ask her if we may take a peek.

Dear Juliet.
How's life? I really liked your house, but I don't
understand why it has so many bedrooms. Another thing:
why does everyone touch your statue? Perhaps it brings
good luck, I don't know. Well, I wrote on the walls too.
It's great—no one says anything to you. I hope to come
back here with my friends, and if things go well, with
"someone." I like writing to you. Now I'm off to Venice!
Bye,

Valeria G., ANNAPOLIS, MARYLAND

Dear Juliet,

I've always been told that touching the breast of your statue would bring good luck. . . . So far, you're not trying too hard. Please, do something for me too!

Giulia O. , MODENA, ITALY

✥

Dear Juliet,

Would you please work your magic and bless me with a passionate love affair that will last forever? He must be tall, handsome, smart, and he must also have a heart of gold. I don't think I mentioned his "gold" bank account. It would be greatly appreciated.

Love,

Crissi L., TORONTO, CANADA

✥

Dear Juliet,

How can you find romance in a cold climate? Per favore!

Susan V., ABERDEEN, SCOTLAND

Dear Juliet,
I want to know why the City of Verona marries its
citizens in love at your tomb, where love died, rather than
under your balcony where love was born?

Giancarlo C., Treviso, Italy

❧

Hello!
My name is Magda. I'm sixteen years old. I have one
big problem. It is very hard for me to find a boyfriend.
I am too impatient and serious. I don't want to be very
obtainable for young men. What should I do? My dream
boyfriend is very simple and poetic. He must be gentle,
clever, honest and brave. Perhaps it's too much for me. If
somebody has the same problem, please write to me. I will
await your answer.
Goodbye.

Saligorsk, Belarus

My dear Juliet,

I am writing to you on Valentine's Day, but unfortunately I don't have a Romeo and I am very sad. I'm not a young girl, but a woman who will turn fifty next March. I've always loved very deeply, but who knows why they have all betrayed me? I hope that after so much suffering, sacrifice, and compromise that I too can be truly happy. I hug you with much affection and wish all lovers on this day much, much happiness.

Graziella B., Milan, Italy

Dear Juliet,

My name is Mark. I am fourteen. I have been going out with this girl for five weeks. Usually my relationships end within two days. She is in eighth grade and is a cheerleader. I really want to kiss her and she wants to kiss me too. We were talking about it one day. What should I do? I also think you should break up with Romeo and go out with someone else. You can pick.

Sincerely,

Mark R., Toledo, Ohio

Eager to heighten the authenticity of our experience, the guard opens a window and tells us to listen to the gypsies' music. "Just like when Juliet lived here," she says.

The fourth floor, up a steep stairway, contains an unexpected mix of objects. Snow White's Seven Dwarfs, fashioned into chunky stools, stand sentry in front of the fireplace. Across a small hallway a larger room holds several cases of medieval and Renaissance pottery from the city's museum collections, much of it crafted during Shakespeare's lifetime. The ceilings are fancifully painted with stars.

By now, it's almost noon and the courtyard is jammed. At least three different tour groups, in as many languages, are getting the inside scoop. Shrieking teenagers take turns giving Juliet a feel; their antics inspire the crowd, and in a matter of seconds it's an impromptu show featuring a steady stream of laughing tourists rushing up to grab or rub the statue's breast.

Though this mildly bawdy scene is amusing, it's time to head for Romeo's house. A right turn onto Via Cappello takes us past the statue of the poet Berto Barbarani, author of an early twentieth-century version of *Romeo and Juliet* in Veronese dialect, and into Piazza delle Erbe, site of the ancient Roman Forum and now an active marketplace where vendors hawk fruit, flowers, postcards, and souvenir T-shirts from stands set up beneath huge canvas umbrellas.

Another right turn down a narrow street, near the pharmacy, leads to Piazza dei Signori, also known as Piazza Dante. And there he is, fashioned in marble, larger than life and deep in thought. It's quite possible that he's trying to resolve a canto in his "Divine Comedy," or he may be contemplating what this piazza will look like once the city completes its extensive renovations.

Across the piazza on the right are the spectacular Arche Scaligere, or della Scala family tombs. Installed behind a wrought-iron fence bearing the della Scala coat of arms and abutting the exquisite twelfth-century church of Santa Maria Antica, this is no ordinary cemetery. Several of the clan rest here in imperial style, elevated above the masses, halfway to heaven. It's hard to choose, but the most fantastic monument may belong to Cangrande I.

Held aloft by four dogs (Cangrande translates as "Big Dog"), his tomb forms a porch over one of the church's doors. Above the tomb, a statue of the ruler reclines on a stone divan. On top of that, astride a marble canopy, sits a copy of the remarkable statue of a beatifically smiling Cangrande on horseback. The original is now at the Castelvecchio Museum.

A few steps past the monument and a right turn put you on Via Arche Scaligere. Romeo's house is here, next door to the casual Ristorante Arche. The street is narrow, and coming on the heels of the della Scala tombs the structure at first appears fairly nondescript. Yet on closer inspection the house begins to tell its story.

Just above eye level, a plaque—"O, Where is Romeo?"—confirms the location, as does the painstakingly exposed brick facade. The impressive front door sports an enormous iron knocker that incorporates the della Scala coat of arms. It has been soldered closed, probably to keep inquisitive tourists from trying to gain entry. A looming

Letters to Juliet

An Herbal Remedy
Gone Wrong?

Believed to be the victim of either intentional or accidental poisoning at age thirty-eight, Cangrande I della Scala was officially exhumed
for the second time, in 2004, and his remains examined. The initial
disinterment, in 1921, revealed a naturally mummified corpse wrapped
in precious gold-infused silks. It did not yield, as the sponsoring party,
an heir to Dante Alighieri, had likely hoped, the original text of
"Paradise."

Sophisticated CAT scans and laboratory analyses carried out during this latest exhumation showed traces of *Digitalis purpurea* (fox-
glove) in Cangrande's feces and liver. While the herb, in diluted form,
was recognized for its diuretic potential during the Middle Ages, its
toxic effects at higher dosages were also well known. It's still a mys-
tery whether his death was due to a mistakenly prescribed overdose
or poisoning by one of his many enemies. Whatever the cause, within
a year of Cangrande's demise, his doctor was arrested and hanged.

security camera momentarily breaks the medieval mood. A twenty-first-century family does live here, after all.

It's mid-afternoon and the street is quiet. A Spanish tour group has just arrived, and the guide is reciting a scholarly history of the myth. We move closer. She doesn't appreciate our eavesdropping and snaps, "This is a *private* tour!" We say, "Of course, didn't mean to intrude," and duck into the herbalist's shop directly across the street from the house.

Along with a few requisite Romeo items, including an extremely sugary cologne, the shop is jam-packed with products from various

Letters to Juliet

monasteries. When we ask the proprietor, a small round man with a bad cold and a great sense of humor, if he has anything that could produce a simulated death, he doesn't miss a beat and recommends the grappa with hot red peppers. As we leave, grappa in hand, we notice the front door of Romeo's house open just a crack and watch as an elegant woman in a wool coat and dark glasses slips out and into a waiting car.

If you love Shakespeare, don't leave Verona without placing a flower on the tomb of Juliet.

ALFRED DE MUSSET, 1847

The tomb is next. Of the sites related to the legend, it's the least trafficked. This may be because of its location, just beyond the city walls on Via del Pontiere, a brisk fifteen-minute hike across town from the houses. Whatever the reasons, you should not be deterred. The first thing you'll notice is the setting. Surrounded by hastily constructed post-World War II buildings, the site has the quality of an apparition, a vision from another age.

A prewar iron sign molded in the shape of a medieval banner incised with the words "Tomba di Giulietta" tells visitors they are in the right place. We walk toward the cloister along a gravel pathway that cuts through a wide expanse of lawn and skirts a now-shuttered kiosk that in warmer months sells souvenirs. From here the path

veers gently to the right and then continues beneath a vine-covered portico after passing a recently installed bronze bust of Shakespeare and a small stone fountain, one of several that lined the original entrance.

At the end of the path, to the left of a building that at one time contained a tobacco laboratory, is a modern addition, part of the efforts during the late 1960s to revitalize the area severely damaged by the 1944–45 bombings.

We pay our admission fee and make a mental note to tour the convent's west wing, home since 1973 to the city's Fresco Museum, dedicated to Giovanni Battista Cavalcaselle, the Veronese art histo-rian and preservationist who salvaged important frescoes from build-ings damaged by floods or destined for demolition. Civil marriages take place here, in the Sala Guarienti, a room lined with exquisite sixteenth-century frescoes by Paolo Farinati. A romantic alternative to city hall, the space is booked months in advance. Natives as well as a large contingent of foreigners recite their "I do"s on the half hour, Thursdays and Saturdays.

For now we make a bee line for the deconsecrated church of San Francesco. Here, tucked behind one of several alcoves displaying an

exceptionally fine survey of Veronese painting from the sixteenth through eighteenth centuries, is a shallow, high-ceilinged chapel with a diamond-patterned stone floor, three delicate lunette windows, and decorated stuccowork. It's not hard to imagine that this is where Friar Laurence is said to have married Romeo and Juliet and, a few days later, handed Juliet the potion. It's a logical choice, given the chapel's likely proximity to the crypt.

To get to the tomb today, visitors must first exit the former church and pass through the interior courtyard. It's a lovely space, intimate and a touch melancholy. In the waning afternoon light it's easy to envision white turtledoves circling and the now-patchy garden overflowing with blooming rosebushes. Ettore Solimani, the man behind this quixotic Eden and Juliet's first secretary, lived here with his family in a wing of the cloister that is now undergoing restoration. An antique stone well, filled with coins from around the world, sits in the center of the garden.

Along the back wall of the courtyard, next to the staircase leading to the crypt, in the spot where Solimani once placed the stand that held his guestbook, is a bronze panel by the Veronese-born artist

Sergio Pasetto. Created in the style of the majestic San Zeno doors, each of the panel's twelve reliefs illustrates a scene from the legend. Directly opposite this work, at the top of the stairs, is the alcove that held Juliet's first mailbox.

A short descent down eighteen brick stairs takes us into a kind of antechamber. It's appropriately cold and damp, and the faux tombstones underfoot impart a persuasive gloom. We duck our heads to pass under the vaulted doorway into the room holding the sarcophagus.

There it is, raised a foot or so off the ground on a stone pedestal, a scrawny plastic bouquet at one end. It overwhelms the small space, illuminated only by three dim bare bulbs and weak daylight. The rough, reddish marble betrays centuries of wear and tear, and the hollowed-out interior certainly suggests a final resting place. A few teenagers appear. Sweetly respectful, they whisper and giggle silently, capturing one another's images on their cell phone cameras. "Where are you from?" we ask. "Rome," they reply in unison and, giggling some more, head up a second staircase that leads directly to the cloister above. We stick around for a few more minutes to scan several notes lying in the sarcophagus. They seem generally more reverential in tone than those left at Juliet's house.

Juliet. Rest in peace with your Romeo. Your love is endless.

✧

Chère Juliette,
Here you found the love of your life. If you can, help me
find where my Romeo is hiding!

✧

Juliet,
Rest in peace, you brave soul. I admire your strength.
Love is yours forever.   *Lily*

✧

Dear Giulietta,
We are Giovanna and Marco and we are in love. With
this note we say hello to you and Romeo and we want to
say we hope our great love will never end. Baci!

✧

Ciao Giulietta,
If you introduce me to Leonardo DiCaprio I will love
you, too!

Urban Archaeology

Few visitors to the tomb are aware that its current, subterranean location dates only to the late 1930s. The first historical reference to the stone artifact, written in the mid-sixteenth century, describes a much earlier relocation from a convent wall to an open courtyard. Later writers describe its installation under a covered arcade and the city's decision, at the end of the nineteenth century, to give it more dignified surroundings.

Where, exactly, was it placed? And how many more times was it moved? We know that if we look hard enough, the cloister will reveal the story of the roving sarcophagus. We have some tantalizing

clues—a stack of old postcards on loan from a Veronese collector and a handful of others found recently by chance at a local fair. And we have Ettore Solimani, Jr., the son of Juliet's first secretary and a witness to the tomb's move to its present spot. He has a few theories of his own and directs us to a large gate near the crypt entrance that leads to a passageway. It is closed and secured with a heavy chain.

So we exit the cloister and walk around the adjacent convent, recently converted to an outdoor exhibition space. We follow the wall around the corner and reach a fenced-in lot with remnants of former walls and little else. It's unclear if this area was damaged during the war or, later, by a wrecking ball. As we flip through the postcards, and try to ignore the territorial Labrador on the other side of the fence, the past suddenly snaps into focus. The sole wall still stand-

ing, distinguished by a low curved niche, a tall window-like opening, and a large rectangular recess, is without question the same brick backdrop visible in one of the early-twentieth-century images of the tomb. In this shot the recess holds inscribed marble tablets and the niche is behind what looks like a guestbook, set on a stone pedestal. The tomb itself rests on a stone slab in the center of the space.

We look at an even older, late-nineteenth-century postcard of the site and there's the wall again. And there's the tomb, shoved lengthwise against it, surrounded by fragments of old columns. While its earlier placements can only be approximated, based on written documents, our photographs confirm that the humble relic's real estate improved with every move.

It's time to leave the crypt. The dank chill is becoming oppressive. As we reach the top of the stairway we hear laughter and shouting. "Auguri!" "Evviva la sposa!" It's a wedding party, emerging from the fresco museum. There's the bride, a froth of white satin and tulle, arm-in-arm with her nattily turned-out groom. Behind the newlyweds are two sets of beaming parents trailed by a dozen or so jubilant guests. They're here because it's beautiful, of course. They're here also because of Juliet. Her unfortunate end has been transformed into hope for new beginnings. She is, after all, a universal symbol of eternal love, and her grip on the imagination is absolute—to the multitudes who throng to her house and tomb and, most of all, to the thousands upon thousands who write her letters.

Dear Juliet,

Even the air is different here. Unlike where I come from, there is room for great emotions. The weekend in Verona was fantastic, even if I was alone, and wanted to be alone. I walked for hours without satiating my desire to see, to feel, to hear. . . . I kept coming back to your house. I wanted to dance in that marvelous room with the fireplace, but I didn't have the courage to do so because people kept coming in. I saw a house for rent on one of the nearby streets and thought how crazily wonderful it would be if I could just stay here, sit down in the great piazza of the Arena and watch the families stroll by. Your house is a huge treasure, and surely Verona must thank you for it, for the fact that humanity can think of you and your story and believe, a little bit, that you protect their love.

Hanna R., COLOGNE, GERMANY

Il Bacio (OIL ON CANVAS), FRANCESCO HAYEZ, 1859